AF521627

THE WAY HOWE TO LYMNE

THE FRIENDS OF THE VICTORIA AND ALBERT MUSEUM

The Friends of the V & A receive the following privileges:

Friends: £15 annually

Friends: (Concessionary) £10 annually for pensioners and full-time Museum staff

Free and immediate entry to all exhibitions with a guest or husband/wife and children under 16

Free evening Private Views of major exhibitions and new developments within the Museum

Quarterly mailings of Museum literature and News Letters

The opportunity to participate in trips abroad with Keepers from the Departments

Discounts in the Craft Shop and on exhibition catalogues

Corporate friends: £100 annually

Receive all the privileges offered to Friends, plus a fully transferable Membership Card

Benefactors: £1000 donation, which may be directed to the Department of the donor's choice

ASSOCIATES OF THE VICTORIA AND ALBERT MUSEUM

The Associates of the V & A are companies who pay a minimum of £500 annually, covenanted for four years, and who take a particular interest in the Museum and have a close involvement with it

Associates
B.A.D.A.
The Baring Foundation
Bonas and Company Limited
Christie's
Commercial Union Assurance plc
Granada Group
Charles Letts (Holdings) Limited
Mobil
The Oppenheimer Charitable Trust
S J Phillips Limited
Rose and Hubble Limited
J Sainsbury plc
Sotheby's
Thames Television Limited
Sir Duncan Oppenheim
Mrs Basil Samuel

Benefactor friends
Sir Duncan Oppenheim
Mr Garth Nicholas

Corporate friends
Asprey and Company
Bankers Trust Company
Bonhams London
Colnaghi and Co
Coutts and Co, Bankers
Doulton and Company
Goldsmiths Company
Madame Tomo Kikuchi
John Keil Limited
Ian Logan Limited
Madame Tussaud's
Mendip Decorative and Fine Arts Society
Barbara Minto Limited
Phillips Auctioneers
Societe Generale
South Molton Antiques Limited
Spink and Son Limited
The Wellcome Foundation Limited

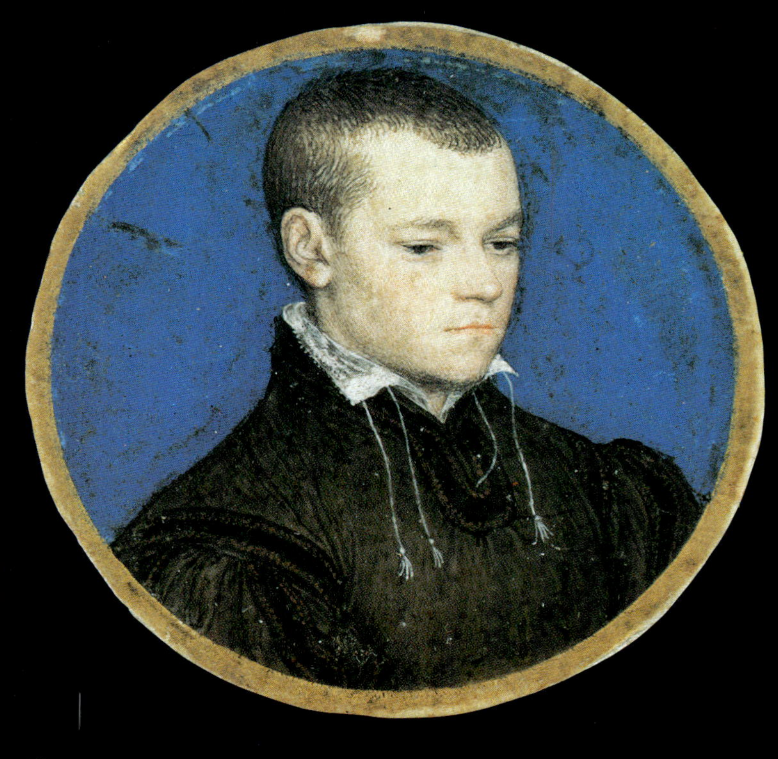

The Way Howe to Lymne

TUDOR MINIATURES OBSERVED

by

Jim Murrell
DEPUTY KEEPER
DEPARTMENT OF CONSERVATION

This book has been published
to accompany the exhibition
Artists of the Tudor Court:
the portrait miniature rediscovered 1520–1620
held at the Victoria and Albert Museum
9 July–9 November 1983

VICTORIA AND ALBERT MUSEUM

Published in 1983 by the
Victoria and Albert Museum,
London SW7 2RL

ISBN 0 905209 39 7

Designed by John Mitchell
Printed in Great Britain by
BAS Printers Ltd, Over Wallop, Hampshire

CONTENTS

FOREWORD
by Sir Roy Strong FSA

The serious study of early English portrait miniatures is a relatively new one. As a subject it can be said to have started under a cloud. The first people to study them in the nineteenth century were collectors and antiquarians. In the case of Queen Victoria and Prince Albert and of the 5th Duke of Buccleuch their collections were an expensive form of grangerising and were certainly not formed from an aesthetic viewpoint. Inevitably this approach, born of the English obsession with faces, diminished their status and the work of Hilliard and Oliver was not seen as being in any way that differet in its premises from that of their successors, Cosway or Smart two centuries later. The fact that these tiny objects are so eminently collectable has been on the whole to their detriment as far as any in depth art historical analysis of them is concerned. The diminished status of miniatures is reflected in the fact that to this day they are invariably sold in sales of objects of *vertu*. In other words for most people they are still bracketed with scent bottles, snuff boxes and similar bijouterie.

The first important contribution to their study was Carl Winter's *Elizabethan Miniatures* published in 1943, a book which exerted a powerful spell over my own imagination. It was not, however, until 1947, when an exhibition organised and catalogued by Graham Reynolds was staged at the Victoria & Albert Museum, that the subject began to be further opened up to academic study. For the first time recognition was given to their unique position as this country's prime contribution to the art of the renaissance. Although the exhibition covered Isaac Oliver as well as Hilliard, it was the latter whose work captured the public imagination, reflecting accurately the tastes of the post-Modernist period. This uncritical adulation has continued ever since. During the 1950s and 1960s the field was opened up further by an examination of the surviving documentary evidence. This was pioneered by Noel Blakiston in a series of articles in the *Burlington Magazine* and summed up in Erna Auerbach's monograph on Hilliard which appeared in 1961. The recent further work on manuscript evidence by Mary Edmond published in the *Walpole Society* (1981) can be said to have rounded off this approach. Important though this work is, it has its limitations. The fact that an artist was a salaried officer of the crown gets us no further in trying to establish what his *oeuvre* was or its meaning in wider terms.

This was quite clear by the opening of the 1970s when it was evident that new ways into the subject were needed. This book is about one of those ways, a study of the technical processes whereby these early portrait miniatures or limnings were actually painted. For this there was an abundance of material in the form of the actual objects themselves plus several manuscript treatises, including Hilliard's *Art of Limning*, which had been published as long ago as 1912, in which the limners recorded how they painted them. No one, however, had actually married the two together. This may be said to be the essence of Jim Murrell's work but from it a great deal of other fact began to emerge which soon enabled the reconstitution of the work of Henry VIII's limner, Lucas Hornebolte, a redefinition of Holbein's *oeuvre*, tentative attributions to the lady miniaturist, Levina Teerlinc, in addition to a reassessment of the work of Hilliard and Oliver. This is a task which I have shared over the past decade as we have studied in the V & A's Conservation Department the majority of the surviving miniatures. Although our approach to the subject is in some ways different, the results in both cases have been the fruit of a lively interchange of views and ideas. We hope that our respective contributions to the study of the art of limning may be at least a stride forward providing foundations upon which a new generation of scholars can build.

PREFACE

The title of this book 'The Way Howe to Lymne' was originally used by John Gwillim in his sixteenth century manuscript compilation of artists' techniques. The explanatory sub-title is my own. These titles do not follow the sequence of the book because I thought it kinder to the reader that he should be gently exposed to the historical and technical survey of Part I before tackling the complexities of the artists' workshops, the 'mechanics' of the limner's art, in Part II.

This book is not a history of early English miniature painting, but intended as integral to its understanding. The study of artists' techniques is essential for an appreciation of the works and their development, and adds enormously to the pleasure we derive from them. And what is art history if it is not about enjoyment?

But for Sir Roy Strong I would never have written this volume. It was he who initiated our studies of sixteenth century miniatures, and over the years I have been a happy collaborator, sustained by his enthusiasm, his peerless knowledge of the field, and by his wit and good humour. It has been a privilege to share in this long and exciting project which has yielded Sir Roy's 'The English Renaissance Miniature', the major V & A exhibition 'Artists of the Tudor Court' and this, my own contribution. Naturally, Sir Roy is not responsible for any errors of fact or interpretation which have occurred in the latter. Among my colleagues at the Museum I owe a great debt to John Murdoch, Deputy Keeper of Paintings, who, like Sir

Roy Strong, has appreciated the contribution which the study of techniques can make to the history of miniature painting. Jonathan Ashley-Smith, Keeper of Conservation, and his predecessor, Norman Brommelle, have supported my forays into the history of artists' techniques, on the grounds that these are legitimate activities for a conservator. I would also like to thank Garth Hall, Stephen Calloway and Anne Buddle who have been closely involved in the research project and who have rescued me from errors which might otherwise have crept into this book. Sally Chappell, of the V & A Photographic Studio, did the photographs with customary skill and cheerfulness.

It was inevitable that the research which is the basis of this book would have involved a great many people outside the Museum. I would like to express my gratitude to those owners/custodians of miniature collections who have made it possible for me to inspect the miniatures in their care and also those who have been prepared to share their knowledge with me. Some have been able to do both, but I list here both owners/custodians and collaborators. My thanks also to those who wished to remain anonymous.

The Royal Collection: Sir Oliver Millar, the Hon. Mrs Jane Roberts

The Collection of HRH Princess Juliana of the Netherlands; Mr A. F. Ubbels

The Duke of Buccleuch and Queensberry, K.T., The Earl of Dalkeith

The Ashmolean Museum, Oxford: Mr David Piper, Mr Gerald Taylor
Miss Janet Arnold
The Countess Beauchamp, K[1]

The British Library, Department of Manuscripts: Miss Janet Backhouse
Major R. J. Berkeley
Mr Robert Bayne-Powell

PHOTOGRAPHIC ACKNOWLEDGEMENTS

Plates 2, 3, 11, 14, 15, 20, 21, 26, 27, 28, 59, 71, 77, 83, 86, 95, 99 are reproduced by gracious permission of Her Majesty The Queen; plates 19, 89, 103 by gracious permission of Her Royal Highness Princess Juliana of the Netherlands; plates 35, 38 by permission of The Countess Beauchamp, K[1]; plates 29, 30, 31, 32, 100, 107 by permission of The British Library Board, Department of Manuscripts; plate 87 by permission of the Trustees of The British Museum, Department of Prints and Drawings; plates 4, 5, 6, 9, 10, 18, 45, 48, 68, 70, 105 by permission of The Duke of Buccleuch and Queensberry, K.T.; plate 92 by permission of Lady Victoria Leatham and the Governors of Burghley House Preservation Trust; plate 88 by permission of the Earl of Powis; plate 42 by permission of Emmanuel College, Cambridge; plates 1, 49, 56, 72, 78, 82, 90, 104 by permission of The Syndics of the Fitzwilliam Museum, Cambridge; plate 73 by permission of Mr. Brinsley Ford; plates 52, 53 by permission of Mrs. Eleanor Hamilton; plate 54 by permission of the Kunsthistorische Museum, Vienna; plate 50 by permission of the 'Mauritshuis', The Hague; plate 75 by permission of the National Maritime Museum, Greenwich; plate 36 by permission of The National Trust, Waddesdon Manor; plate 40 by permission of The Public Record Office; plate 81 by permission of the Rijksmuseum, Amsterdam; plate 80 by permission of The Royal Museum of Fine Arts, Copenhagen; plates 7, 8 by permission of the Collection V de S; plate 13 by permission of The Wallace Collection; plate 39 by permission of The Dean and Chapter, Westminster Cathedral; plates 34, 66 by permission of the Yale Center for British Art, Paul Mellon Collection, New Haven, Connecticut.

PART I

The Technical Evolution of the Portrait Miniature

IN THE SEVENTEENTH CENTURY miniatures were frequently referred to as 'paintings in little', a term which should be reserved for those small oil portraits on metal such as Eworth's Mary I[1] (Pl. 105). In the eighteenth century Walpole was obsessed with the magnification of miniatures claiming that 'the largest magnifying glass only called out new beauties from Elizabethan Hilliard's Olivers works'[2], and that 'if a glass could expand Samuel Cooper's pictures to the size of Vandyck's they would appear to have been painted for that proportion'[3]. Such comparisons suggest that limning is no more than scaled-down easel painting. Nothing could be farther from the truth. Limning, said Hilliard, 'is a thing apart from all other *Painting* or *drawing* and tendeth not to comon mens usse'[4]. Limning was 'a thing apart' because it had its own special purpose, its own very unusual and demanding techniques and its own colour scale. During the sixteenth century it was not for common men's use. Until Hilliard was forced by financial circumstances to open his studio to any (wealthy) client the commissioning of portrait limnings was virtually a royal prerogative.

There is a danger in making a belittling comparison of miniatures with oil paintings, for their size is only relative to their purpose and does nothing to diminish their artistic quality. As Graham Reynolds wrote '. . . minuteness in itself is of no aesthetic merit. It is true but irrelevant, that the miniatures of Hilliard and Oliver reveal fresh merits under the strongest lens; that sureness of touch and skill of eye are revealed by the most meticulous inspection. If they had revealed no other merit, they would take their place with those who can write the Lord's Prayer on a grain of rice, as mountebanks of art'[5].

---

1. Hans Eworth, *Mary I.* Oil on gold, circular, 56 mm diameter. Collection of the Duke of Buccleuch.
2. Horace Walpole. *Anecdotes of Painting*, 1762. Vol. I, p. 154.
3. Ibid., Vol. III, p. 61.
4. Nicholas Hilliard, *The Arte of Limning*. Ed. R. K. R. Thornton and T. G. S. Cain, 1981, p. 62.
5. Graham Reynolds. Nicholas Hilliard and Isaac Oliver, 2nd Ed., 1971, p. 19.

The technical evolution of the portrait miniature

The term 'miniature' has nothing to do with smallness but reflects its technical descendence from the art of book illumination[6]. Not every miniature is small enough to be held in the palm of the hand and many are larger than small oil paintings or other examples of graphic art. The only proper definition of miniature painting is in terms of its specialisation and minuteness of technique; a technique which is common to no other type of painting and which appears flawless even on the closest observation.

In limning the art and the craft are inseparable and this is central to its proper understanding and appreciation. If the limner failed to master the technique he failed as an artist[7].

Various origins and influences have been proposed – from Roman portrait medallions and an isolated portrait enamel by Jean Fouquet to the Renaissance revival of the classical medallion. But if we consider limning in the light of a technical evolution the development can be traced from its origins in the illustration studios of the Ghent-Bruges school through a studio tradition which encompassed the works of Horenbout, Holbein, Levina Teerlinc and latterly those of Hilliard and Oliver. The mastery of the craft was passed on from master to pupil in a continuous studio tradition.

Contemporary art historians have attributed certain miniatures of Henry VIII, which evidently pre-date the images of Hans Holbein, to a member of the Horenbout family. The miniature which was central to this development is the portrait of Henry VIII which is now in the Fitzwilliam Museum (Pl. 1), tentatively attributed to Lucas Horenbout (now frequently known by the anglicised version

---

6. The word 'miniature' is derived from the medieval latin *miniare*, to embellish a manuscript with minium, red lead. The best account of the development of the word in a wider European linguistic context is contained in *Aspects of Miniature Painting* by T. H. Colding, 1953, pp. 9–19.
7. It is not a paradox that many of the finest miniatures were quite freely executed. The freedom of artists such as Holbein and Oliver is always contained within the rigid framework of the inherited limning technique.

of his name: Hornebolte) by Carl Winter[8]. In 1953 Colding produced a compelling argument for attributing that miniature to Horenbout[9]. The most progressive published work to date on the *oeuvre* of Lucas Horenbout is that produced by Graham Reynolds in 1956[10], where a number of other miniatures were grouped around the Fitzwilliam portrait on stylistic grounds and attributed to the same hand. The works which Reynolds considered to be comparable with the Fitzwilliam *Henry VIII* were two circular miniatures of the same sitter in the Royal Collection (Pls. 2 and 3) and another in the collection of the Duke of Buccleuch (Pl. 4). He also included a limning of *Henry, Duke of Richmond* at Windsor (Pl. 11), a portrait of a man, called *Thomas, Earl of Essex*, sold from the Sotheby Collection in October 1955, and an *Unknown man*, now in the Mellon Collection at Yale, although this has recently been demonstrated to be by Hans Holbein.

Since 1976 a number of miniatures, clearly related to the

---

8. Carl Winter, *The British School of Miniature Portrait Painters*. Proceedings of the British Academy, Vol. XXXIV, London, 1948, p. 7. See Hugh Paget, *Gerard and Lucas Horenbout in England*. Burlington Magazine, November 1959, pp. 396–402. On p. 399 there is a summary of the earlier literature on Horenbout.
9. T. H. Colding. *Aspects of Miniature Painting*, Copenhagen, 1953, pp. 63–5. Colding confused his argument and sadly weakened his otherwise sound case by including with the Fitzwilliam miniature a replica at Windsor Castle which he asserted was by the same artist. The miniature in question has long been regarded as a late copy and has recently been attributed to the nineteenth century miniaturist-antiquarian, George Perfect Harding. The reason for Colding's error seems to have arisen from a misreading of Chamberlain (Arthur B. Chamberlain, *Hans Holbein the Younger*. London 1913), from whom he quotes a passage (p. 55) as evidence of Chamberlain's linking of the two miniatures. In fact the passage does not refer to the Windsor replica but to two circular miniatures of Henry VIII also in the Royal Collection. In a later passage (Chamberlain II, p. 234), in which he discussed the Fitzwilliam portrait, then in the Collection of the Duke of Buccleuch, Chamberlain made it perfectly clear that he regarded the Windsor version as a copy and that he had no illusion about its antiquity. The miniature is a poor copy, painted in techniques quite different from those of the original.
10. Graham Reynolds. Portrait Miniatures, Connoisseur Guide, The Tudor Period, 1956, pp. 127–135. See pp. 128–129.

Fitzwilliam *Henry VIII* have been examined at the Victoria and Albert Museum from both the technical and stylistic standpoint. In 1978 it became possible, through the generosity of their owners, to examine a group of ten such miniatures together at the Museum. This pilot group consisted of the Fitzwilliam *Henry VIII*, the two portraits of *Henry VIII* from the Collection of H. M. the Queen and the further portrait of *Henry VIII* from the Collection of the Duke of Buccleuch[11]. There were no less than three portraits of *Katherine of Aragon* (Pls. 5 and 6), as well as portraits of *Charles V*, of *Mary Tudor*, and of a lady called *Jane Seymour* (possibly Anne Boleyn) (Pl. 9). An eleventh miniature was examined but was rejected on both stylistic and technical grounds[12].

This group was also subjected to a rigorous technical examination, using microscopy[13], tangential light[14], ultra-violet fluores-

---

11. The four miniatures of Henry VIII were included by Graham Reynolds in his pioneer grouping of Horenbout miniatures.
12. Margaret Wotton, Marchioness of Dorset. Circular 35 mm diameter. Painted in watercolour on vellum stuck to plain card. Collection of the Duke of Buccleuch.
13. The use of the microscope in the technical examination of miniatures is normally limited to magnifications of between ×7 and ×40. Occasionally magnifications of over ×100 may be used to observe the particle characteristics of pigments. The microscope reveals clearly the calligraphic brushwork used in the flesh and other areas of miniatures. It helps to make accurate assessments of the modes of paint application in various techniques and, to some extent, of the layer structure of the painting. It is also of value in detecting areas of damage or restoration. Idiosyncratic brushwork and techniques are recorded for comparative purposes by colour macro-photography.
14. Tangential light is used in conjunction with the microscope; the paint surface is examined while it is illuminated by a narrow beam of light which strikes it at an angle of incidence of 5°. This reveals the slightest variations in the relief of the paint surface. Although this method is of greater value in the examination of mid-to-late-seventeenth century miniatures in which the brushwork, especially in the features, became thicker and 'impasted', it is occasionally useful in detecting on the smooth surfaces of sixteenth century miniatures the presence of thicker restorations. This method is also capable of detecting the absence of a true carnation ground, its presence being essential to the acceptance of a miniature as having been painted in sixteenth or seventeenth century England.

cence[15], infra-red reflection[16] and X-radiography[17]. On all counts the ten miniatures ascribed to Lucas Horenbout were demonstrated

15. Ultra-violet fluorescence has long been used in the examination of many kinds of works of art for the detection of repairs, restorations and forgeries, and occasionally to view writings and drawings which have become invisible to the naked eye (see Jane Roberts and Carlo Pedretti, *Drawings by Leonardo da Vinci newly revealed by ultra-violet light*. Burlington Magazine, Vol. CXIX, pp. 396–408). The technique is used in the examination of miniatures to detect areas of restoration, paintwear or damage. It is particularly useful in revealing the anachronistic use of zinc white (a pigment which was not generally adopted for miniature painting in this country until c.1830) in restorations, fakes or late copies. Zinc white, even when mixed in quite small quantities with other pigments, has a characteristic acid-yellow fluorescence under ultra-violet light. Frequently the works of an individual artist can be recognised because of their consistent and characteristic pattern under ultra-violet light.
16. The piece of equipment used for the infra-red examination of miniatures is an infra-red image-converter. It uses the invisible infra-red band of the light spectrum to produce an infra-red 'picture'. It does not make a permanent image; for this a photograph taken on infra-red sensitive film must be used (Joyce Plesters, *Painting Methods and Materials: A Brief Survey of Published Work from 1961 to 1972*. In *The Conservation and Restoration of Pictorial Art*, Ed. Brommelle and Smith, 1976, pp. 3–5. See p. 4 and notes). Although infra-red light in the examination of paintings is used to penetrate the paint layers and reveal the underlying drawing in carbon, or to enhance the images of worn inscriptions or drawings, its main use in the examination of sixteenth century miniatures is its ability to distinguish between the two bright blues, ultramarine (lapis lazuli) and bice (azurite) which were used for painting backgrounds. Because it was virtually impossible to obtain lapis lazuli, even towards the end of the century (and then only at great cost), any miniature which has an ultramarine background, and which purports to be of an earlier date, must be regarded with some suspicion (see R. D. Harley Artists' Pigments c.1600–1835, 1970, pp. 41–47). Only a few sixteenth century miniatures have so far been discovered which have ultramarine backgrounds and the majority of these can be demonstrated to have been painted in c.1600.
17. X-radiographs have been used for many years in the examination of easel paintings. Their application is normally in the detection of underlying evidence of the structure of the painting and its support, of changes of design on the part of the artist, and in the revelation of complete paintings over which later works have been executed. The use of X-radiographs in the technical study of miniature paintings is systematic and they are studied for an entirely different reason. Pilot studies of X-radiographs of characteristic and well-authenticated works by various miniaturists have shown that idiosyncratic X-ray patterns are distinguishable due to the use and distribution on the paint surface of various pigments. These patterns generally vary considerably

to be from the same hand. A number of other miniatures have been examined separately, using the same techniques, and have also been attributed to the same artist. Two of the miniatures inspected were of exactly the same size and from their format were intended to be seen as a pair, depicting *Henry VIII* at a rather later date than the portraits of the King which have been discussed, with a pendant portrait of his grandmother, *Lady Margaret Beaufort* (Pls. 7 and 8). Another miniature which has been scrupulously examined is that of *Edward VI* at the age of about four years (Pl. 10) and which, although it has been trimmed to an oval shape, is certainly a portrait of Edward before he succeeded to the throne by Horenbout, and was probably painted from life. The portrait of Henry Fitzroy, Duke of Richmond (Pl. 11), which Graham Reynolds included in his list of miniatures attributable to Horenbout, was similarly scrutinised and was revealed as one of the finest by the artist. Another exciting recent find is a later miniature by Horenbout of *Henry VIII* which, although certainly influenced by Holbein's image of the King, was painted in the naturalistic and sympathetic manner which is so characteristic of Horenbout's portraiture (Pl. 12).

The portrait of *Holbein* (Pl. 13), formerly described as a self-portrait, has recently been catalogued by Graham Reynolds as being the work of Lucas Horenbout[18]. It was not possible to make a complete examination but the miniature was inspected by × 10 magnification, by ultra-violet light, and with the infra-red image converter. Although the hatching of the features is rather more closely-wrought than that of the most of the miniatures examined it is very close to the remainder of the group of Horenbout. The features are certainly the same as those of the Holbein self-portrait drawing at the Uffizi[19]. If that *is* a late image of Holbein the miniature must be a copy of a *self-portrait* for, as Sir Karl Parker pointed out, on the basis of

from artist to artist because of their individual employment of the various pigments available during given periods.

18. Graham Reynolds, *Wallace Collection, Catalogue of Miniatures*, 1980, pp. 33–39.
19. See Exhibition Catalogue, *Firenze e L'Inghiterra, Florence*, Florence, 1971, No. 40.

his bias towards top-left to bottom-right diagonal hatching in his drawings, Holbein was a left-handed artist[20], and the portrait in the Wallace Collection (and the other versions) is the *mirror-image* of a left-handed painter. Therefore the Wallace miniature must be a copy by Horenbout after a lost *self-portrait* by Holbein, which could well have been a miniature.

The examination of the miniatures attributed to Horenbout showed them to have a number of identical characteristics, some more or less common to all early sixteenth century miniatures, but others painting to a single artist with his own mannerisms and methods. The former, more generalised, methods were to become standard in later English portrait limnings. The miniatures were painted with watercolours on thin vellum which was stuck to a piece of card, almost invariably cut from a playing card. With two exceptions, the rectangular Fitzwilliam *Henry VIII* (Pl. 1) and the Buccleuch *Katharine of Aragon with a marmoset* (Pl. 6), the miniatures are circular in form, and even in the Fitzwilliam miniature the portrait is set with an inner circle of gold. The features of the sitters were always executed with transparent hatches over a smooth, opaque ground, which in later writings on miniature painting was described as the 'carnation'. In most of his miniatures Horenbout used an unusually warm pink for the carnation and always modelled the features over it with transparent hatches of red and grey. The modelling of the heads is in soft gradations of tone, as if they had been seen in a very diffused light, and there are no hard edges as there are in the works of Holbein and Hilliard. The features are characterised by a certain mannerism in the modelling of the eyes and mouth, giving the former a heavy, pouched appearance and making the latter full and red. The hair was always worked in dark lines over a middle tone and was frequently heightened in lines of opaque colour. All the backgrounds were very smoothly floated with copper blue (almost

---

20. K. T. Parker, *The Drawings of Hans Holbein in the Collection of His Majesty the King at Windsor Castle*. London, 1945, p. 32.

certainly the pigment prepared from the mineral azurite and known as 'blue bice') while the costumes were in a middle-tone and were sensitively modelled in transparent darks and opaque lights mixed from the basic colour. Hilliard underlined the importance of this type of shadowing and heightening, using the same colour as the middle-tone; '*Paulo Lamatius* in the last chapter of his fowerth bouck very truly (but absurd) sheweth that every thing must be shadowed in his kind. . .'[21]. Occasionally, the costumes were beautifully diapered with gold or other colours. The use of gold in these miniatures is important in comparing the miniatures of Horenbout with the illustrations of the late Flemish book illustrators. The gold was always applied as a powder in the same way as a pigment, bound with a watercolour medium. Where it was used to represent jewellery it was applied over a dark ochre ground, but for the gold lines which encompass the miniatures it was painted directly over the vellum. In no case was the gold burnished to give it a metallic sheen. Gemstones were rendered with opaque colours, while pearls were painted with thick opaque grey, with highlights of white. There are idiosyncracies in those miniatures which have gold inscriptions, invariably in Roman capitals. A peculiar type of curved 'X' was used and the diagonal stroke of the 'N' was sometimes reversed (Pl. 1)[22].

In the light of van Mander's assertion that Holbein was instructed in the techniques of miniature painting by Horenbout[23], we should expect Holbein's miniatures to be painted in methods similar to those above. In 1977 eight miniatures from Carl Winter's fastidious short-list of those attributable to Holbein[24] were compared in detail at the Victoria and Albert Museum[25]. The conclusion was

21. By 'absurd' Hilliard evidently meant that Lomazzo had stated the obvious.
22. For a comprehensive list of the miniatures now attributed to Horenbout see Sir Roy Strong *The English Renaissance Miniature*, Chapter 2.
23. Carel van Mander, *Schilderboek*, 1604. Translated by Constant van der Wall, New York, 1936, p. 89.
24. Carl Winter. Burlington, Vol. LXXXIII, 1943, pp. 266–269.
25. The miniatures examined were:
    (a) Anne of Cleves (b) Mrs Pemberton

that they were early sixteenth century works by an extremely gifted artist who, on stylistic grounds, could not be confused with Horenbout, and could be Hans Holbein (Pls. 14, 15, 16, 17, 18, 20, 21). At the beginning of 1978 the miniatures of William and Margaret Roper from the Metropolitan Museum were examined in detail and were also attributed to Holbein, as, recently, have several others (Pl. 19) as can be seen by consulting Sir Roy Strong's list[26]. The works of Holbein and Horenbout can only be differentiated by style, by the calligraphic treatment of the features and by the relative breadth and competence in the handling of the costume, so extraordinarily similar are their techniques.

Holbein's miniatures are also painted with watercolour on vellum stuck to card, frequently cut from a playing card. The miniatures are all circular. The features are modelled in transparent grey and red (or occasionally brown) hatches over an opaque pink carnation ground. Although Holbein sometimes used a carnation which was as deep as those of Horenbout, he usually varied the tone according to the complexion of the sitter[27]. The treatment of the hair, the floated blue bice backgrounds, the handling of costumes and the use of unburnished gold over brown ochre for jewellery, and directly over the vellum for the edge-lines, recall Horenbout. But Holbein's hatching is more regular and disciplined, being concentrated in significant areas of internal form, often breaking into longer lines at the overlapping edges of forms and at the contours, creating a controlled linear interpretation of the third dimension which is remarkably similar to the graphic technique of his portrait drawings (Pl. 23). The result is a more refined and dignified, but less intimate and naturalistic, type of portraiture than that of Horenbout. The overall design of

---

(c) Catherine Howard
(d) Lady Audley
(e) Henry Brandon
(f) Charles Brandon
(g) Catherine Howard
(h) Lord Abergaveny

26. Sir Roy Strong, *op. cit.*, Chapter 3.

27. The features of the Brandon brothers, for instance, are modelled over comparatively pale carnations.

Horenbout's miniatures is weaker and although the two artists used the same opaque handling in the costumes, Horenbout's approach is that of the conscientious book illustrator, appearing finicky in comparison with the intuitive breadth of Holbein's work[28].

Carl Winter wrote: 'His (Hilliard's) technical and stylistic descent from artists whom we may conveniently personify in Horenbout, and thence through Holbein, provides the main link between his art and fifteenth century book-illumination'[29]. In Winter's day there was no opportunity to make the rewarding comparative technical studies of the works of Horenbout, Holbein and Hilliard which have recently been carried out. Stylistically the works of Holbein and Hilliard are poles apart; technically the link is very slender even when Hilliard copied Holbein[30]. What exactly did Hilliard mean when he wrote '*Holbeans* maner of *Limning* I have ever Imitated, and howld it for the best. .'[31]? Hilliard wrote those words in about 1600 when he was painting the flattering and bedazzling portraits of Elizabeth, shimmering with imitation jewels and bright colour, which cannot bear comparison with the grave, searching portraiture and controlled simplicity of design which characterise Holbein's work in miniature. Hilliard meant that he had seen and admired miniatures by Holbein. This is substantiated by the inscription of the sitter's name on Holbein's miniature of *Lord Abergaveny* (Pl. 18), which is surely in Hilliard's distinctive calligraphy. Hilliard could not have learnt the specialised techniques of limning from an examination of Holbein's works. It must be assumed, therefore, that he was instructed by an artist who practised miniature painting between the

28. For an example of Holbein's greater virtuosity in the handling of costumes compare the shot silk effect in green and brown in his Henry Brandon (Pl. 15) with Horenbout's awkward attempt at a similar effect in the sleeve of the portrait of Henry VIII in the Buccleuch Collection (Pl. 4).
29. Carl Winter, *op. cit.*, pp. 7–8.
30. Two of the four miniatures which Hilliard executed for the Bosworth Jewel were copied from prototypes by Holbein (Henry VIII and Jane Seymour).
31. Hilliard, *op. cit.*, p. 68.

death of Horenbout and the emergence of Hilliard's early mature works, which were painted in the Anglo-Flemish manner inherited from Horenbout.

This artist was most probably the court miniaturist Levina Teerlinc, who had been appointed on Horenbout's death as Henry VIII's *paintrix* and who had worked for every succeeding monarch until her death in 1576[32]. So the similarities in Hilliard's early works of the 1570s[33] with other sixteenth century miniatures were those which Graham Reynolds described as 'inessential' for miniatures attributable to Horenbout[34]. The vellum was stuck to card and the features were painted with transparent hatches over a carnation. The carnation was much paler than those of Horenbout, Holbein and Teerlinc and the hatches were an imitation of the burin technique of engravers such as Dürer[35] (Pl. 24). A smoothly floated, azurite blue was normally used for the backgrounds and the costumes were executed in opaque body-colour.

However, his miniatures of the later 1570s display many techniques which reflect his background as a goldsmith; his interest in precious metals and stones and the relationship of the portrait miniature with a jewelled setting. He was using powdered silver and gold, not as metallic pigments, but as surrogates for areas of polished metal such as the armour and gold jewels of his sitters, by burnishing them with a polished tooth when dry. The gold lines around the edges of his miniatures were not applied over the bare vellum, but were painted thickly over the other colours and burnished, as were the calligraphic gilt inscriptions. His treatment of jewels was not calculated to imitate their appearance so much as to produce minute

32. It is interesting that the notion that Teerlinc was Hilliard's tutor was suggested at the same time from three independent sources; the editors of *The Arte of Limning*, Sir Roy Strong, and myself.

33. Hilliard's *juvenilia* have been excluded at this stage because of their debatable status in his *oeuvre*.

34. Graham Reynolds, *op. cit.*, pp. 128–129.

35. Nicholas Hilliard, *op. cit.*, p. 101.

counterfeits on the surface of the miniature[36]. Hilliard's obsession with real surfaces and textures did not stop with jewellery. He also washed his white pigments to make three different grades, to be used for imitating various surface textures, and he employed an unusual number of black pigments for the same reason[37]. Such techniques, with their emphasis on the reproduction of jewels and metals and the surface texture of fabrics, and their insistence on brilliance of colour are, of course, ideally suited to the integration of the miniature with an elaborate jewelled setting; but they have nothing in common with Holbein, who was only concerned with reducing the scale, design and tonal range of his easel painting style to make his work acceptable 'in little'.

Hilliard was not therefore especially influenced by Holbein's techniques or entirely by his style. The only features which the two artists share are their linearism and avoidance of heavy shadows. In

---

36. Hilliard's treatise is the first which dealt with the problems of portrait miniature painting. There are earlier manuscripts and one printed book which discussed the materials and techniques of miniature painting, but they were concerned with the decoration of books rather than the painting of portraits. The works concerned are the book entitled *The Arte of Limming* of 1573, and the manuscripts *The Waye Howe to Lymne*, etc., c.1582, in the Victoria and Albert Museum Library, the British Library Manuscripts Sloane 122, which is datable c.1500, Sloane 3292, the origin of the contents of which is c.1564, Harley 1279, which is pre-1600 in origin, and Stowe 680, which was probably written c.1600. It is unlikely that there was any previous text on portrait miniature painting, or Haydocke would not have been so insistent that Hilliard should commit his knowledge to paper: '. . . for (to speake a truth) his [Hilliard's] perfection in ingenuous Illuminating or Limning, the perfection of Painting, is (if I can judge) so extraordinarie, that when I devised with my selfe the best argument to set it forth, I found none better, then to perswade him to doe it himselfe, to the viewe of all men by his pen; as hee had before unto very many, by his learned pencell: which in the ende hee assented unto; and by mee promiseth you a treatise of his owne Practise that way, with all convenient speede'. Giovanni Paolo Lomazzo. *A Tracte Containing the Artes of Curious Paintinge Carvinge and Building*. Translated by Richard Haydocke, London, 1598, p. vi.
37. Hilliard, *op. cit., passim*. Norgate, British Library MS. Harley 6000, *passim*. British Library MS. Harley 6376, *passim*.

the *Arte of Limning* Hilliard did not acknowledge this debt to Holbein, although he did stress the importance of line and the ruinous effect of heavy shadows in miniature painting. But even their linearism differs. Hilliard's portraits seem flat while Holbein's are rounded in spite of their linear qualities. It is almost certain that Hilliard did not see the evidence of Holbein's graphic working methods contained in the 'great booke' of drawings, which at the time seems to have been sequestered in the collections of the Earl of Arundel and of Lord Lumley[38]. Had Hilliard done so the direction of miniature painting in the late sixteenth century might have been profoundly altered. Perhaps the easiest way to appreciate the difference between the linearism of Holbein and Hilliard is to adopt Nicolaides' arbitrary distinction between the terms 'contour' and 'outline'[39]. It is useful to contrast Hilliard's outline which was inflicted upon the *internal forms*, with Holbein's emphasis on a *contour* which resulted from their careful study.

Hilliard, in the *Arte of Limning* writes: '. . . let that your first lyne be the forehead stroake, as for exampel [regarding a linear sketch in the margin]. Soe then you shall proceed by that scalle or scantlinge to doe all proportionablye to that bignes, as if the forehead be but so longe, then the rest of that lyne to the chine is but twice so long, as thus [referring to another marginal drawing], and so proceed still, weel marking when yo loosse that line, that is to say, when that lyne is not to you, to your seeing, as when you first sawe it and drue it, for then your mark is remembered, which you shall best knowe and perceive by the distance betweene the eye and that lyne, howe neare it or howe fare.'[40]. It is quite clear that Hilliard was relating all the internal forms of the features to one, duly proportioned

38. *Holbein and the Court of Henry VIII.* Catalogue of an exhibition at The Queen's Gallery, Buckingham Palace, 1978–9, p. 11.
39. Kimon Nicolaides. *The Natural Way to Draw*, London, 1972, pp. 12–13. 'We do not think of a line as a contour unless it follows the sense of touch, whereas an outline may follow the eye alone.'
40. Hilliard, *op. cit.*, p. 80.

line. Earlier in his *Arte of Limning* he had proposed rather crude rules of perspective for the recession of the features, rather than obser-vation of their relationships, one to another, '. . . the furthest eye from the drawer must be a littel hig[h]er than the hethermost, becosse of the perspective, if the drawer sit any deall hig[h]er then the party drawne, but if lower, then the further eye must be a littel lower; if leavel, then to be of one hight.'[41]. Hilliard also recorded what is certainly the most obvious weakness of his own approach to draw-ing in the following passage, '. . . but the littele moving [of the sitter] leadeth to a great error if you perceive it not quickly, soe that they sometime make the eyes at one position or standing, the nosse at ane other, the mouth at an other, the eare at an other.'[42].

The advantage of drawing the internal forms first and gradually relating them to a contour is that the early work may be fairly loosely drawn and slight movements of the sitter may then be accommodated in the drawing. It is evident from Hilliard's *Treatise* quoted above, as it is from his miniatures, that his approach to drawing was to establish a firm outline and to relate the internal forms and shading, or hatching, to it. It is this approach which is largely responsible for Hilliard's geometric interpretation of form and his two-dimensional treatment of pictorial space, although it may be that this was his deliberate, personal interpretation of the linearism which is so apparent in the works of Holbein. However, deliberate or not, there is a great deal of difference between the flat, hard linear abstractions of Hilliard's work and the three-dimensional simplicity which was the result of Holbein's feeling for the inter-relation of form and contour.

On the basis of the vivid graphic development of Holbein's drawings at Windsor he evidently worked to no preconceived out-line, but began his portraits by exploring the interior forms and

41. Ibid., p. 78.
42. Ibid., p. 80.

planes, gradually extending them until he arrived at a linear contour.[43] The exhibition *Holbein and Court of Henry VIII* provided an excellent opportunity to make a study of a major part of the 'great booke.'

Ganz thought that the drawings were originally executed in chalks only and that all the inked contours were the result of restoration. Parker suggested that the inked contours might be the result of either later corrections by Holbein himself, an imbalance produced by the abrasion of the chalks, or the result of the artist's use of a tracing apparatus such as that described and illustrated by Dürer[44] (Pl. 25). But why should Holbein have used a strong ink line for tracing when he intended to finish the works with subtle and sensitive interior modelling with chalks? Holbein's drawings were never intended as objects for display but were working notations intended for use as studio material in the production of finished easel paintings and miniatures. The weight of some of the contours may be due both to the corrections made by the artist and to the erosion of the chalk drawing[45].

Perhaps the most revealing of Holbein's drawings is that of *Mary, Duchess of Richmond and Somerset*[46] (Pl. 26) which, as an unfinished work, shows the early stages of one of his portrait drawings. If this drawing is contrasted with that of an Unknown Lady[47], which is a finished version of the same time of female portrait, one can visualise Holbein's earlier loose working of the internal forms of the features which were gradually hardened in relation to the contour, which was the result of their formal relationships in space. Thus

---

43. K. T. Parker, *op. cit.*, *passim*, Holbein, Queen's Gallery, *op. cit.*, *passim*.
44. Parker, *op. cit.*, p. 28.
45. Holbein, Queen's Gallery, *op. cit.*, *passim*.
46. Ibid., No. 35 (Parker 16). This drawing, which has been described as worn but not retouched, does not seem to have been recognised as an unfinished work. Had it been completed and its present state was the result of wear we should expect traces of the original, deeply incised, contour lines. There are none.
47. Ibid., No. 43 (Parker 47).

in a number of drawings there is a great deal of very faint internal modelling in red chalk which does not seem to serve any real purpose in the final contoured working drawings.

The portrait of *Sir Thomas Perry*[48] is a typical example of this inconspicuous internal drawing. The inner modelling on the shadowed side of the nose establishes the left contour, while its relationship with the other contour is carefully established by faint modelling hatches, feeling their way across the forms of the lighted side of the face to arrive at the turning and disappearing planes which create the contour at the right.

Two further drawings are cited which probably demonstrate Holbein's approach to drawing more clearly than any of the others. The first drawing is of *Sir Henry Guildford*[49] (Pl. 27), in which the modelling hatches curve away from the nose, the mouth and the chin, their hooked ends following the disappearance of the planes and creating a contour which does not rely on the establishment of a single line, but which is the result of the turning of the planes at the extreme visible edge of the forms of the face. The other drawing is that of *Sir Richard Southwell*[50] (Pl. 28), where the finalised contour of the back of the neck has been established over the disappearing curved modelling hatches of the muscles.

Apart from a few basic miniature painting methods, common to all sixteenth century limners, the portraits of Hilliard are, paradoxically, related to those of Holbein only by a misunderstanding, or disregard, of his approach to linearism.

The most obvious clue to the book illustrator's background of the artist whose works have been attributed to Lucas Horenbout is the decorated border of the Fitzwilliam *Henry VIII* (Pl. 1), where angels are 'censing' the linked initials of the King and his Queen,

48. Ibid., No. 71 (Parker 81).
49. Ibid., No. 12 (Parker 10).
50. Ibid., No. 23 (Parker 38).

Katharine of Aragon. The background colour of the border is vermilion which, like the blue backgrounds of this and other portraits, is very smoothly floated. The angels are drawn in lines and hatches of gold over a brown ochre ground. Although this may seem a slender clue to the 'Flemish connection', it is an extremely valuable one, for the prototypes for the border and angels can be found in the decorated books of the Ghent-Bruges school. Such angels, with long oval faces, painted either in polychrome or in the 'gold over brown ochre technique', abound in the works of the late Flemish illuminators, their archaic form seeming slightly at odds with the naturalism of that school. They might have fluttered from the panels of Memling or Van der Goes.

A Book of Hours in the British Library[51] provides a number of valuable links with both the drawing of the angels in the Fitzwilliam *Henry VIII* and the techniques of their execution[52]. In the first few folios containing the Kalendar there are central panels in the borders containing figures representing the occupations of the Months; these are carried out in gold lines and hatching over a brown ochre ground and are alternately placed against smooth floated backgrounds of vermilion and ochre. A few pages later in the same book there is a *trompe l'oeil* border of carved wood screening represented with gold drawn over a brown ochre ground surrounding a painting of the Crucifixion. The painting within the border is arched at the top, forming two spandrels containing angels almost identical to those in the Fitzwilliam miniature[53] (Pl. 29). In another Book of Hours the borders to the Kalendar contain medallions of Saints which are drawn in gold over ochre with the same crispness which

51. The purpose here is to ignore the scattered works of the Tudor Royal atelier and link the portraits of Horenbout directly with the works of the Ghent-Bruges school of illuminators.

52. British Library MS. Additional 35314, ff.1–5. (T. H. Colding, *op. cit.*, remarked on the similarity to the Fitzwilliam angels.)

53. Ibid., f.8.

typifies the angels of the Fitzwilliam *Henry VIII*[54]. The same book has a border where figures painted with gold lines and hatches over brown ochre are placed against a smoothly floated ground of vermilion[55]. Such decorative treatment of figures and angels is commonplace in the works of the late Flemish illuminators and a number of similar examples can be seen in what is probably the best known work of the Ghent-Bruges school, the Grimani Breviary[56].

The most characteristic technique of early English portrait miniatures is that of painting the features with touches of transparent colour over an opaque carnation ground; and it was to endure in miniatures painted on vellum for two hundred years after the earliest works of Horenbout. This was considered to be so exclusively *English* in origin, that Norgate could write in 1648, 'Tis true the Italians use noe grounds atall but worke the Complexion upon the bare parchment without more adoe, but the English as they are incomparably the best Lymners in Europe, soe is their way more excellent, and Masterlike Painting upon solid and substanciall body of Colour much more worthy Imitation then the other slight and washed way'[57]. And imitated it was, for at about this time a Parisian court miniaturist was laying a ground on his vellum in imitation of the methods of the Englishmen Samuel Cooper and Peter Oliver[58]. Hornebout frequently used an unusually deep pink carnation in comparison with those of the later artists, apart from Holbein who often used a similar colour. It seems possible that Holbein's adoption of a deep pink ground for the portrait drawings which he executed

---

54. British Library MS. Additional 35313.
55. Ibid., f.43b.
56. Biblioteca Marciana, Venice.
57. Edward Norgate. Miniatura. Ed., Martin Hardie. Clarendon, 1919, p. 20.
58. André Felibien. *Entretiens sur les vies et sur les ouvrages* des plus excellens peintres. Paris, 1672–1688, Part V, p. 55. 'Hanse couchoit due blanc sur son velin, & cherchoit a imiter la maniere d'Olivier & de Coupre qui travailloient avec estime en Angleterre.' Hanse, or Hans, was a soubriquet for Louis van der Bruggen, a pupil of Simon Vouet who died at Paris in 1658.

during this second visit to England may have been influenced by his contact with Horenbout.

In the naturalistic paintings of the Ghent-Bruges school of illustrators light is all important; it is a diffused light which models the forms gently by subtle changes of tone and colour rather than by using shadow. Many of the figures are too small to provide useful comparisons for Horenbout's portrait works but they usually have a warm pink ground over which other colours are washed in order to produce their impressionistic modelling. Colding pointed out that a bust length picture of *Christ* in a Book of Hours in the British Library[59] has a strong technical affinity with the Fitzwilliam portrait of Henry VIII, remarking that 'the face is underpainted with a strong flesh colour over which the features have been modelled with grey and red strokes'. Colding might also have commented on the soft colour transitions with which the head of Christ is modelled and with its parallel in the similar treatment of lighting in the Fitzwilliam miniature. In this and other heads of a similar scale in late Flemish book paintings there is a trait which is not entirely consistent with the portrait works of Lucas Horenbout. This is the use of opaque heightening touches in the features. Although Horenbout did employ this technique in two of his miniatures; the poignant portrait of the sickly *Henry FitzTudor* and that of *Edward VI* as a child, he normally modelled the features with transparent grey and red over the carnation. The general absence of highlights in his miniatures is because his figures do not have to relate to landscape lighting, for the naturalistic heads are isolated within their intense blue backgrounds.

In the same book recalling the Fitzwilliam *Henry VIII* there is a figure of *Christ in Majesty*[60] (Pl. 30) painted in red and grey hatches over a warm pink ground, which also has some opaque

59. Colding, *op. cit.*, pp. 64–65. The picture of Christ occurs in British Library MS. Additional 35314, f.79.

60. British Library MS. Additional 35313, f.8.

heightening touches. Many of the smaller figures in this book have features which are modelled in transparent hatches of red and grey over a warm, pink carnation[61] and in some cases, such as the Annunciation[62], no opaque heightening has been used. The features of numerous figures in the illustrations of a prayer book of the early sixteenth century are painted in the same technique[63]. The Book of Hours of the Infanta Juaña of Spain provides an example of a portrait proper, where the Infanta is depicted at prayer with an angel and her patron saint, John the Baptist[64] (Pl. 31). The portrait not only displays the expected techniques in the painting of the face, but also has the softness and delicacy of modelling, and the naturalistic but sympathetic representation of character evident in Horenbout's portrait of *Katharine of Aragon with a marmoset* (Pl. 6).

The other trademark of sixteenth and early seventeenth miniaturists was floating very smooth backgrounds with the heavy and coarse pigment blue bice, made from the mineral azurite. This method was frequently used in the paintings and border decorations of the Ghent-Bruges school[65].

Horenbout's techniques for painting goldworks, jewels and pearls are mirrored in the naturalistic illustrations of the Ghent-Bruges school and the *trompe l'oeil* borders of jewellery so often used to surround their works[66]. His techniques for depicting jewellery can be seen time and again in the borders and pictures of the books of the late Flemish masters.

---

61. British Library MS. Additional 35314, *passim*.
62. Ibid., f.12b.
63. British Library MS. Egerton 2125, ff.64b, 142b, 146b, 154b, 157b, 174b, 186b, 194b, 200b, 212b.
64. British Library MS. Additional 18852, f.26.
65. Grimani Breviary, *op. cit.*, ff.2–13; British Library MS. 35313, f.56b, f.213b, f.217b, f.224b, f.231; British Library MS. Additional 35314, ff.2v and 3, ff.4v and 5; British Library MS. Additional 38126, f.13.
66. British Library MS. Additional 38126, f.67; British Library MS. Egerton 2125, f.142v; British Library MS. Additional 35314, ff.72v and 74; British Library MS. Additional 35313, f.8, f.223b, f.224, f.225, f.231b, f.232, f.235b.

A Flemish 'portrait' type

There is an important piece of evidence cutting across the arbitrary boundaries created by Colding which have obscured the origins of the portrait miniature. (Colding insisted on a firm division between what he described as 'cabinet' and 'decorative' miniatures[67]. 'Cabinet' miniatures, he argued, were square or rectangular in form and were a development from the art of book illustration; while the 'decorative' miniature, which was circular or oval in shape, was dependant for its development on the demands of the art of the goldsmith. Colding carried this rule to a *reductio ad absurdum* by describing the Fitzwilliam *Henry VIII* as a 'cabinet' miniature because of its rectangular shape[68]. It could well have originally been set in a jewel or mounted in an ivory box, as were so many circular and oval sixteenth century miniatures which Colding would have described as 'decorative'. He also mentioned the famous reference to Susanna Horenbout in Dürer's diary of 1521, when that artist admired and purchased from her a *Salvator Mundi*[69], which Colding assumed was a 'cabinet' miniature because it was referred to as *ein Blättlein*, although that only tells us it was painted on a small, loose leaf, presumably of parchment. The painting could have been of any shape and may even have been laid on card.) There is evidence of a separate 'portrait' miniature type emanating from the Ghent-Bruges school in a Book of Hours previously mentioned[70]. In one of the typical *trompe l'oeil* borders hangs a pendant oval miniature in a fairly simple gold locket, which was evidently intended to be worn as a piece of costume jewellery. The painting is a bust-length picture of Christ in naturalistic colours with a flat blue background; certainly a work executed with watercolour on vellum (Pl. 32).

A characteristic of Horenbout's portraits, which is stylistic rather than technical, is the tendency to emphasise the modelling

67. Colding, *op. cit.*, Chapters 1–4.
68. Ibid., pp. 63–66.
69. Ibid., pp. 60 and 63.
70. British Library MS. Additional 35313, f.231b.

of the eyes, giving them a 'pouchy' appearance, and to make the lips full and red. These mannerisms have many precedents in the works of the late Flemish illustrators.

The dating and iconography of Horenbout's miniatures are evidence that Henry VIII continued to employ him to portray members of the Royal family long after the arrival at Court of the cosmopolitan and more prestigious artist, Hans Holbein. Henry's preference for Horenbout is also shown by his higher salary, in spite of Holbein being chosen to travel abroad to depict the King's prospective brides and to execute the great wall-painting at Whitehall. Perhaps Henry's loyalty to Horenbout is explained by his indifference to Holbein's cold Mannerist portraits, though they were recognised as an expression of his prestige as a great European monarch, and by his affection for the naturalism of the unpretentious portraits of the closest members of his family. He said of Horenbout: 'For a long time I have been acquainted not only by reports from others but also from personal knowledge with the science and experience in the pictorial art of Lucas Horenbolte. .' If Smollet's account of Henry's reaction to Anne of Cleves is not apocryphal[71], then perhaps Holbein may have been better at painting idealised images than he was at the traditionally elusive art of 'catching a likeness'.

After the sudden deaths of Holbein and Horenbout within a few months of each other, the early Anglo-Flemish miniature painting tradition was sustained by the slender talent of Levina Teerlinc until the emergence of England's first native-born limner, Nicholas Hilliard, in the early 1570s. Because of the absence of any signed or authentically documented works by Teerlinc there has never been a serious attempt to separate her works from the few undistinguished miniatures which survive between 1544 and 1571.

Contemporary documents reveal that she was the most prominent limner during that period, serving four monarchs from Henry

71. *The Oxford Dictionary of Quotations*, p. 242. 'The King found her so different from her picture . . . that . . . he swore they had brought him a Flanders mare.'

VIII's later years until well into Elizabeth's reign. She painted for Elizabeth for several years after Hilliard's emergence and his first official portrait of her in 1572. In spite of Terrlinc's evident importance as a court limner she was not prolific. However, if a *corpus* of fine miniatures from between 1544 and 1571, connected with the court, could be selected and shown to have sufficient technical and stylistic characteristics in common to demonstrate that they were the work of a single artist, then that artist must be Levina Teerlinc. Such a group of works does exist and, although the miniatures have the same general technical features as those of Lucas Horenbout, the brushwork is different and is closely related to that of Levina's father, Simon Benninck, another scion of the late Ghent-Bruges school of book illustrators.

The characteristics which distinguish Levina Teerlinc's works from those of her predecessors in the Anglo-Flemish portrait limning tradition are mainly those of style and competence, rather than of basic technique. She usually adopted a circular format, painting on vellum stuck to card, working the features transparently over a carnation and floating the backgrounds with blue bice. She executed the goldworks of jewellery with powdered gold pigment over ochre and painted the encircling gold line of her portraits over the bare vellum, just as Horenbout and Holbein had done. However the appearance of her works is quite different largely because of her loose, washy, almost impressionistic, treatment of the features, also evident in her father's *Self-portrait*[72] (Pl. 37).

It is unfortunate that few of her miniatures have escaped the attentions of nineteenth century restorers who painted carefully over the faces, probably in an attempt to smooth and prettify Teerlinc's rather brusque and broad treatment of the features in her portraits.

Her draughtsmanship was poor and led to grotesque enlarge-

72. There is another miniature portrait which (from a photograph) could plausibly be attributed to Benninck. It is a portrait of an *Unknown Man*, Musée du Louvre, Paris (Sauvageot Bequest No. 1064), illustrated by Colding, *op. cit.*, Fig. 102.

ment of the head in relation to the body and a gauche, angular, emaciated representation of the figure. Her rendering of costume was also inept in comparison with the assurance of her predecessors.

Fortunately several portrait limnings by Teerlinc have survived unscathed by the restorer's brush. These are the *Lady Katharine Grey* (Pl. 33), an *Unknown lady* (Pl. 34), and an *Unknown man dated 1569* (Pl. 35) and another *Unknown man*, depicted within an armillary sphere, also dated 1569 (Pl. 36). The works which have been attri-buted to Teerlinc on stylistic and technical grounds are widely separ-ated in date and cover practically the whole period in which she flourished. Although there are some differences in style due to Teer-linc's eclectic dependence on contemporary influential portraitists these miniatures admirably demonstrate her face-painting method. Instead of the fine hatches of Horenbout and Holbein she worked the features in a more spontaneous manner, using broad washes of colour interspersed with an occasional line to accent a contour. In spite of the difference in technique her rendering of the features has a sympathetic naturalism and suggests a verisimilitude to the sitter which is reminiscent of Horenbout's work. Sadly, the charm of her face-painting is invariably marred by the stiff, puppet-like bodies which she attached to the heads. The figures of her sitters' are usually shown in an awkward full-fronted pose, often with stick-like arms akimbo.

The relationship of Teerlinc's portrait works with those of her father can be clearly demonstrated by a comparison of the miniatures discussed above with Simon Benninck's *Self-portrait* of 1558 (Pl. 37). Although it may seem strange that four successive monarchs should have elected to use Levina Teerlinc, who was quite obviously inferior to her predecessors, she was probably the best they had, like Charles II's inadequate Lely[73].

73. According to Jonathan Richardson, Lely was asked by a friend, 'For God's sake, Sir Peter, how came you to have so great a reputation? You know that I know that you are no painter.' To which Lely replied, 'My Lord, I know I am not, but I am the best you have.'

From contemporary records of her productions and from the attributable works, it seems that Levina Teerlinc was more involved in painting illustrative works directly derived from the Ghent-Bruges tradition (whether as separate miniatures or paintings within illuminated books) than Horenbout and Holbein. The most important detached work in this genre which can be attributed to her on grounds of style, technique and artistic incompetence is the *Elizabethan Maundy* (Pl. 38), which has unfortunately been cut down from its original rectangular format to an oval. Such works were often given as New Year Gifts and would have been expected, certainly by Elizabeth, from a person such as Levina, who was a 'gentlewoman' of the Court (the sort of position to which Hilliard aspired but was unable to attain). More important are some paintings which are incorporated into illuminated books and an illustrated Plea Roll.

The earliest book illustrations which can be firmly attributed to Teerlinc on grounds of style and technique are some paintings in Mary Tudor's Manual at Westminster Cathedral. The 'Manual' is devoted to two obligatory services which had to be performed by the monarch; the 'Blessing of the Cramp Rings' and the 'Laying on of Hands for the King's Evil' (Pl. 39). Each of these ceremonies provided Teerlinc with an excuse to paint pictures which contain portraits of Mary Tudor and others in an architectural setting.

The features of Mary Tudor in these illustrations are painted in Teerlinc's familiar loose, washy manner, as are the portraits of others in the ceremonies. The architectural settings are not inventions but are convincing studies of actual interiors. They are carried out in the Bennick style but with less competence. These illustrations can be directly compared with a work by Benninck in an incomplete Book of Hours in the Victoria and Albert Museum[74], where a paint-

74. Victoria and Albert Museum Library. Purchased at Christie's, New York, May 22nd, 1981, Lot 10. Ex-collection of Eric Sexton.

ing of the 'Mass of the Dead'[75] includes similarly painted naturalistic faces against a carefully observed architectural background.

Teerlinc's unmistakable style and techniques are also evident in some later illuminated documents. In the illustration within the illuminated 'P' of the Plea Roll for Michaelmas 1553 we see Teerlinc at her best – confident and completely at home in the Ghent-Bruges tradition of the landscape with figures. The landscape and the broad, impressionistic, opaque handling of the figures find direct parallels in a series of sample Kalendar paintings by Simon Benninck[76]. The angels in the scene are of the familiar Flemish type.

Levina Teerlinc may have taught Hilliard the techniques of decorative illumination, as well as the art of limning. If Hilliard failed to acknowledge this debt in his book, it may have been because the stigma of having been the pupil of one of Henry VIII's anonymous 'strangers', and a female at that, would have denied his claim to have been heir to the legacy of Holbein. The source for Hilliard's *Queen Elizabeth in robes of State* (Pl. 41) was a pattern created by Levina Teerlinc in illuminations such as that on Queen Elizabeth's Indenture for the Foundation of the Poor Knights of Windsor (Pl. 40). The illumination of the Mildmay Charter (Pl. 42) is without doubt the work of Hilliard and shows his technical prowess. Interestingly the figures at the left side of the capital 'E', containing the portrait of Elizabeth, are strongly reminiscent of figures with which Teerlinc decorated certain borders of Mary Tudor's Manual.

Before examining Hilliard's mature works of the 1570s we must consider the juvenilia; the three works which he is reputed to have painted at the age of thirteen. The attribution of the two self-portraits

---

75. Ibid., f.21v.
76. These consist of two leaves of parchment painted on both sides in the Victoria and Albert Museum Library and two more similar leaves in the British Library. The arrangement of the illustrations for the Months on both sides of each leaf and their random disposition suggest that these pages were intended as examples to be shown to prospective patrons.

to Hilliard cannot be sustained for one is a later copy of the other[77]. They are irreconcilable because a blue-eyed boy of thirteen does not develop into a brown-eyed man of thirty[78] (Pls. 43 and 44). The third miniature, that of *Edward Seymour, Duke of Somerset* (Pl. 45), is probably by the youthful Hilliard, for it is exactly what one would expect from a youth who had potential artistic talent but who lacked any proper training. That this miniature is quite dissimilar in style and technique to any previous limning or to any miniature from Hilliard's subsequent career weighs in favour of the attribution, for the clumsiness of its execution betrays a lack of any training in the Anglo-Flemish tradition, and the strange gold background suggests an ignorance of metropolitan limning conventions. This work supports the view that limning was a skilled art which was handed on in a studio tradition.

It is in the handful of miniatures which Hilliard painted before his extended visit to France that we find some slight substantiation for this claim that he had imitated Holbein. These works have the spareness of technique of the previous Anglo-Flemish miniaturists and also a linearism and simplicity of silhouette more akin to Holbein's miniatures than those of Horenbout and Teerlinc. However the similarity is rather superficial because of Hilliard's non-spatial approach to drawing. Even in his first dated work, the so-called *Oliver St John of Bletsho* of 1571 (Pl. 46), this difference is immediately evident if it is compared with any Holbein limning. However, these miniatures of the early 1570's are more realistic than anything Hilliard subsequently achieved; the delineation of the features is more searching and sensitive. Hilliard's youthful promise was never realised for he allowed his work to ossify into an insensitive and antiquated formula.

---

77. The miniature in the Buccleuch Collection is painted on a seventeenth century 'prepared card' support.

78. Compare this miniature with the self-portrait at the age of thirty in the Victoria and Albert Museum.

A number of other works which he painted during the early 'seventies show great promise and originality. They demonstrate Hilliard's ability as a descendant of the Anglo-Flemish tradition, but reveal an individual approach to portrait limning. There is a pair of a husband and wife painted in a rectangular format rather than the circle which had been consistently used by previous limners (Pl. 47); a carefully drawn *Unknown Lady*, aged 52 (Pl. 48) and the *Unknown Man, aged 33*, formerly in the Heckett Collection, the first adult work Hilliard signed; his first portrait of *Queen Elizabeth*, now in the National Portrait Gallery is from this period. There are two dated works from 1574 which again show Hilliard's freshness and originality. The *Jane Boughton* (Pl. 49) illustrates Hilliard's growing interest in costume and jewels, while the *Unknown Man, aged 37* (Pl. 50) is remarkable for its bright green background. The *Unknown Lady* of 1575 is also a fine example of his early, spare style (Pl. 51).

Although Hilliard employed the basic Anglo-Flemish methods in these early works he had already added a number of technical innovations. Unlike his predecessors he did not paint the gold line around the edge of the miniature on the bare vellum, but applied it thickly over the other paint. This was of less importance than his novel practice of burnishing all the gold used in a miniature into a glittering, metallic smoothness, adding a new decorative brilliance to his works. New also was his technique for painting pearls with a burnished silver highlight over a rounded blob of white lead paint. Perhaps the most striking was his adoption of fine calligraphy and arabic numerals for his inscriptions, in place of the Roman capitals and numerals which had been used by previous artists and which he himself had used for the inscription on the early *Edward Seymour*. The quality of these early inscriptions suggest that at some time between 1560 and 1571 he studied under a master calligrapher.

In two limnings dated 1576 Hilliard used the technique which he invented, and of which he was rather secretive, for representing coloured gem stones by applying an appropriately tinted hot resin over a burnished silver ground. The appearance of the sitters and the identification of one of them as the *Earl of Leicester* indicate that Hilliard adopted this technique before his visit to France. In an early experiment in the *Jane Boughton* of 1574 (Pl. 49) he painted rubies with a red stained resin directly over the vellum. All this leads one to suspect that a very beautiful pair of small portraits representing *Queen Elizabeth* and her favourite the *Earl of Leicester* (Pls. 52 and 53), which were probably once a part of an elaborate jewel, were produced between 1574 and 1576, for both contain rubies carried out in the resin over silver technique, while the Elizabeth is adorned with diamonds executed with burnished silver, another innovation. Once he had perfected a new technique Hilliard made it a permanent part of his repertoire, to be repeated endlessly (and to an extent indiscriminately) throughout his career.

Little survives from Hilliard's sojourn in France between 1576 and 1578. It has been supposed that either Hilliard's father, Richard, travelled to France to be painted by his son in 1577, or that Hilliard returned briefly to England in that year (Pl. 24). However the miniature concerned should be treated with some caution as technical examination suggests that it may have been executed later. The last figure of the date of Hilliard's inscription has been tampered with, suggesting that it was not originally a '7'. The blue background is even more confusing, being carried out with ultramarine rather than blue bice[79]. Ultramarine was so scarce and expensive in the sixteenth century that it was rarely used and even at the end of the century Hilliard suggested substitutes in his *Treatise*. No other miniature prior to the 1590s has yet been discovered in which ultramarine was used for the background. Therefore, this work must be treated as an anachronism and not representative of this stage of Hilliard's career. Three key works may be chosen from Hilliard's French adventure as typical of his limning methods during those years. These are the *Duc d'Alencon* (Pl. 54), the *Self-portrait* of 1577 (Pl. 44) and

79. This was detected by infra-red examination.

the *Alice Hilliard* of 1578 (Pl. 55). They reveal a more flamboyant style and decorative techniques. Hilliard's time in France evidently gave him more confidence in his own powers. This is reflected in his increasingly abstract and schematic approach to the portrait, which soon resulted in the uncompromisingly geometric drawing of the features and the neat, but rather soulless, hatched modelling in the manner of 'some fine well graven portrature of Albertus Dure'[80]. He maintained this schematic and insensitive treatment of the features with little alteration until the end of his working career and dogmatically defended these methods in *The Arte of Limning*. As Auerbach pointed out, Hilliard's adoption of the tall oval format in preference to the circles, rectangles, and the one short oval which he had used previously, also dates from this period[81].

There was little change in Hilliard's techniques during the years between his return from Paris and his death in 1619. The decorative methods which he had invented for the use of gold and the representation of other metals and jewels were retained, and Hilliard's further technical experiments were limited to backgrounds and edges. The most important of these techniques was the substitution of a crimson curtain behind the sitter to replace the traditional blue background. This innovation may have been inspired by the small portrait of *Mary Tudor* by Hans Eworth (Pl. 105). The earliest dated miniature in which he employed this device is the *Sir Henry Slingsby* of 1595 (Pl. 56), although he may have used it earlier in undated works. The technique he employed is best described as 'wet-in-wet', where a darker mixture of the lake colour was floated into a lighter layer which was still damp. After 1600 Hilliard adopted a short-cut to achieve this effect, lifting out the lights with a dry brush from a dark wet ground of lake[82]. This method can be seen in Jacobean miniatures such as that of *James I* (Pl. 57) with an inscribed border

80. Hilliard, *op. cit.*, p. 100.
81. Erna Auerbach. Nicholas Hilliard, p. 27.
82. British Library MS. Harley 6376, p. 52.

and the *Charles I as a youth* (Pl. 58). This latter technique produced crisper and rather angular lights in the background and has a decorative quality which is more in keeping with Hilliard's geometrical treatment of the figure. There were earlier indications that Hilliard was not entirely content with the usual flat blue background, for he attempted in various ways to relieve its monotony. There are a number of works in which he added hatched shadows of darker blue at the lower edges of the blue ground, the earliest of which date from the 1580s. There are also two quite late portraits of *Queen Elizabeth* (at the Victoria and Albert Museum and at Ham House) in which Hilliard attempted to repeat the handling of his crimson curtains in the blue backgrounds. In one of these he first floated the background with the usual blue bice and then used ultramarine to imitate laboriously the crisp shadows of a suspended drapery which had been recently folded and ironed so that it hung in neat squares behind the sitter. The other miniature has the background floated with a blue-grey colour (probably the pigment smalt, which Hilliard had recommended, along with blue bice, as a good substitute for ultramarine), the 'wet-in-wet' technique simulating a loosely hung drape.

After 1580 Hilliard began to take more interest in the decoration of the edges of his miniatures. Usually this resulted only in placing the gold edge-line over an ochre ground, accentuating the brilliance of the burnished gold. Sometimes, however, he would develop the edge into a decorative band, using a gold motif over a brown ochre ground, such as that in a *Queen Elizabeth* at Windsor and later in the *Ludovick Stuart* of 1603 (Pl. 106), where a broad band of ochre at the edge has thin encircling gold lines and a gold inscription. In the *James I* (Pl. 57) the crimson curtain background is encircled with a band of blue bordered with gold lines and containing the inscription. A similar motif appears in the *Charles I as a youth* (Pl. 58) where the edge is painted with a band of smalt and decorated with a gold pattern. Perhaps the most extraordinary example of this extension of decoration into the border is that in the

Charles I as a boy in the Victoria and Albert Museum where the background is floated with blue which is interrupted at the right and left edges by straight vertical bands of gold decoration, while the top edge is extended into a *trompe l'oeil* gold arch. There is little doubt that in producing these borders Hilliard was attempting to create a decorative transition between the miniature and the jewelled locket or picture box; a late attempt to integrate *completely* the miniature and the jewel.

There is a group of miniatures which Hilliard painted at the end of the sixteenth century which deserves particular attention because some of these works have in the past caused confusion over the length of Hilliard's working life. Central to the group are the four which he painted for the Bosworth Field Jewel representing *Henry VII*, *Henry VIII* (Pl. 59), *Jane Seymour* and *Edward VI* which were all copied from earlier works by other artists. The Jewel was made in 1600 or slightly later. Three other miniatures, similar in technique to those of the Bosworth Field Jewel, were painted by Hilliard at about the same time, all derived from images which from the costume pre-date his adult career. These miniatures are the *Unknown Lady*, called *Queen Elizabeth* (Pl. 61), *Edward Seymour, Duke of Somerset* (Pl. 60), and *Queen Elizabeth in Robes of State* (Pl. 41). The costume of the first of these miniatures dates from c.1570 or slightly earlier but the techniques show that Hilliard painted it at the end of the century. The execution of the jewels, the decorative edge of gold over ochre and the use of ultramarine for the background suggest a dating of 1590–1610. The *Edward Seymour*, because of its inscribed date of 1550[83] has been treated as an embarrassing anachronism and has been suppressed with the comforting attribution 'Artist unknown' in spite of it palpably being a work by Hilliard, because its style and technique is identical to the above group. Although *Queen Elizabeth in Robes of State* has always been accepted as by Hilliard it has, because of the Queen's youth and the dating of the

83. The date has been tampered with and the last figure may read '9'.

costume, been placed at the very beginning of the artist's adult career with a putative date of c.1569. On technical consideration it must have been painted much later suggesting that it was derived from a work by an earlier artist, probably Levina Teerlinc. The techniques which place this work so firmly in the later years of Hilliard's career are those which are generally characteristic of this whole group. The features are modelled with soft long hatches and the contours are drawn in the hard, abstracted line characteristic of Hilliard's work in the years after his visit to France. The extensive and developed use of jewel painting techniques also argues the later date. This miniature is unique in Hilliard's *oeuvre*, for among the surrogate jewels, with their deceptive glitter, he has set a real table-cut diamond in the centre of the cross of orb. The final argument for dating this and the other miniatures closer to 1600 is the extensive use of ultramarine in the background.

If there is a certain stiffness about Hilliard's copies it is probably because he was unused to painting at second-hand. He made it perfectly clear in *The Arte of Limning* that his normal procedure was to work *ad vivum* directly on to the vellum. There is absolutely no reason to believe, as Pope-Hennessy suggested, that Hilliard painted his miniatures from preliminary portrait drawings as Holbein had done, and that one day a volume of studies similar to Holbein's 'great booke' will come to light[84]. Hilliard was too confident of his powers as a draughtsman to have felt any need for such studies and his simplified geometric formula for drawing the features would have rendered them entirely unnecessary. The one drawing of Hilliard's which survives, which is not a design, is that of *Queen Elizabeth* (Pl. 62). Although this could be a preliminary drawing for a full-length miniature it seems more likely to have been a preliminary study of one of the Great Seals. It provides good evidence to refute Pope-Hennessy's proposition that Hilliard made use of a mechanical drawing device such as that which Parker suggested that Holbein

84. John Pope-Hennessy, *A Lecture on Nicholas Hilliard*, 1949, p. 26.

might have used[85]. The forms of this drawing are far too symmetrical and geometric to have resulted from a tracing device, and the folds of the costume are drawn in the antiquated 'pot-hook' convention which is far removed from the natural construction resulting from an exact individual copy[86]. The one type of preliminary study we might have found in Hilliard's works and those of Horenbout and Teerlinc, is that which Oliver produced as a painted pattern for portraits which he intended to reproduce in a number of replicas. In Oliver's oeuvre such pattern works are represented by the *Queen Elizabeth* (Pl. 64), the *Earl of Essex* (Pl. 66), and the *Charles I as a youth* (Pl. 65). The absence of such patterns among the surviving works of previous miniaturists suggests that other arrangements were made for the multiplication of images from a sitting. It is possible that on the completion of the first portrait the artist would reproduce the features on a new vellum tablet in preparation for the next commission; a process which could be repeated until a new *ad vivum* portrait was made. Hilliard was renowned for his prodigious visual memory and it seems possible, especially in his repetitions of Queen Elizabeth, that he could draw the features again without recourse to an *aide memoire*[87]. The schematic and spare quality of his portraiture would have made these repetitions less demanding than for artists who worked with closer observation and more developed modelling. This would also partly explain the variable quality of the miniatures of James I. There is no doubt that he was assisted in the mass production of these portraits and it seems probable that Hilliard would

---

85. Pope-Hennessy. Ibid., p. 26.
86. Hilliard, *op. cit.*, p. 84.
87. See Sir John Harington. Ariosto's Orlando Furioso in English Heroical Verse, 1591, pp. 277–8. – 'I thinke our countryman (I meane Mr Hilliard) is inferior to none that lives at this day: as among other things of his doing, myselfe have seen him, in white and black in four lynes only, set downe the feature of the Queenes Majesties countenance: that it was ever hereby to knowne; and he is so perfect therein (as I have heard others tell) that he can set it down by the Idea he hath, without any patterne.'

have drawn the outline of the features on the carnation, leaving the assistant to 'fill in' the outlines with colour and to add the background and costume.

We can be reasonably sure of the identity of two of Hilliard's painting assistants at this time. Certainly Lawrence Hilliard was working with his father and we may assume that Rowland Lockey would have been a willing helper, for there is evidence of his continuing association with Hilliard after the end of his apprenticeship[88].

A putative *oeuvre* of independent portrait miniatures may be assembled for Lockey by comparing works from the large group of limnings which can be generally described as 'School of Hilliard' with the right-hand group of figures which were Lockey's original *ad vivum* addition to his version of Holbein's *The Family of Sir Thomas More* (Pl. 67). Such works as the *Unknown Lady* in the Edward Grosvenor Paine Collection and the *Sir Francis Walsingham* in the Buccleuch Collection (Pl. 68) bear a very close relationship to this group. Lockey's work is characterised by his use of a rather thick carnation with the features modelled in coarse but vigorous vertical brown hatches. His rendering of costume and jewellery was also cruder than that of Hilliard.

Hilliard's enthusiasm for his son's talent expressed in correspondence with Sir Robert Cecil[89] might have been a cynical attempt to get him work but could be a simple case of paternal affection blinding judgement. Lawrence's signed works speak for themselves. They display little artistic ability and less imagination, relying entirely on a strict imitation of Nicholas Hilliard's manner limited by Lawrence's crabbed and timid handling. Lawrence was not even capable of the discipline of hatching, and the naively drawn features of his sitters are modelled with a flaccid stipple, usually in a dirty brown colour (Pl. 69).

Nicholas Hilliard left no talented successor to his style, unless

88. Auerbach. Hilliard, pp. 254–5.
89. Ibid., p. 38.

John Hoskins, who was a skilful exponent of his jewel and fabric painting techniques during the 1620s, was trained in his studio. Even Hoskins, however, used a softer and more volumetric drawing in the features and figures of his sitters and here his work was more closely related to that of his contemporary, Peter Oliver (Pl. 98). Hilliard left no true successor because his manner had outlived its usefulness, superseded long before his death by a demand for the greater realism which resulted in the popularity of his rival, Isaac Oliver. Since the early 1580s Hilliard's career had been distinguished for its total lack of originality (apart from the formulation of a few technical innovations) and for his failure to appreciate progressive pictorial developments such as volume and space, linear and aerial perspective, and the study of anatomy.

Isaac Oliver was a totally different artistic personality. His searching, inventive mind grasped contemporary currents in European art and led to original ideas which enriched his own contribution to the art of limning and provided the foundation for the great developments in miniature painting of the seventeenth century.

In the absence of any documentary evidence it has been assumed, incorrectly, that Oliver served a full term of apprenticeship with Hilliard[90]. This prompted another false hypothesis; that there should be works by Oliver in Hilliard's manner and that they could be found among those normally attributed to Hilliard.

Sir Roy Strong has pointed out that the development of Oliver's artistic personality is best appreciated through his drawings, the earliest of which must considerably pre-date his limnings; evidence that Oliver came to Hilliard not as a beginner but as a fully-fledged artist[91]. However, this should have been evident from a study of Oliver's earliest dated miniatures. The first known limning, the *Unknown Woman, aged 20 in 1587* (Pl. 70), is a daringly original three-quarter length standing figure, an extension of the traditional head and shoulder format, which Hilliard himself had not then attempted

90. Ibid., p. 232.

91. Sir Roy Strong, *op. cit.*, Chapter 6.

in a miniature. In 1588 Oliver followed this with four brilliant and vigorous portraits of men which are quite unlike anything which Hilliard ever produced (Pls. 71, 72, 73). These show an artist aware of the latest developments in Flemish art, who could translate the current graphic style of Goltzius into the terms of a completely new medium. In 1590 Oliver also painted two tender and sympathetic miniatures of children (Pl. 74), their perceptiveness rivalled hitherto only by Holbein's portraits of Henry and Charles Brandon (Pls. 14 and 15). It is unlikely that a youth who from his early 'teens had been subjected to seven years of Hilliard's bigoted and dogmatic instruction could have survived with the independence and education to produce such works at twenty or twenty-two (Pl. 71).

Hilliard can only have passed on to Oliver the techniques of portrait limning. The association must have lasted for a period of no more than a few months, or even weeks, probably during the early part of 1587 when Oliver painted his first signed miniature. Thus Oliver owed no more to Hilliard than had Holbein to Horenbout: again a certain painting 'mystery' was passed from one mature artist to another. We may never know the circumstances of Hilliard's tutelage of Oliver but it is evident in Oliver's miniatures that Hilliard passed on to him his most treasured secret, the technique of making imitation jewels on a minute scale. In view of the barely-concealed materialism of *The Arte of Limning*, it seems likely that Oliver would have paid for this 'mystery' and was indeed a fee-paying student.

Nowhere can the difference in approach and artistic education of Hilliard and Oliver be seen more dramatically than in comparison of their cabinet miniatures. In works such as *Sir Robert Dudley, George Clifford, Earl of Cumberland* (Pl. 75) and *Sir Anthony Mildmay* Hilliard repeated what is virtually the same full-length pose, while in *Robert Devereux, Earl of Essex*[92] (Pl. 76) he avoided a further

92. Although the crudeness of execution of this miniature suggests that Rowland Lockey may have been involved in its production the composition was, without doubt, inspired by Hilliard.

repetition only by reversing the figure. In contrast Oliver seems to have regarded each of his cabinet miniatures as a fresh exercise in composition, never repeating a formula. In each of his major cabinet portraits from the early *Young man, once called Sir Philip Sidney* (Pl. 77) at Windsor, through the circular mannerist paintings of *the so-called Frances Howard* at the Victoria and Albert Museum (Pl. 91), and '*Lucy Harington*' at the Fitzwilliam Museum (Pl. 78), to the unprecedented group portrait of the *Brothers Browne* at Burghley (Pl. 92), the *Baron Herbert of Cherbury* in the collection of the Earl of Powis (Pl. 88) and the full-length *Richard Sackville* in the V & A (Pl. 79), he presented a variety of original poses; while in the *Allegory of Love* in Copenhagen (Pl. 90) he presented a compendium of poses without parallel in Elizabethan art.

Hilliard's cabinet miniatures also display his ignorance of the principles of linear and aerial perspective. His inability to create pictorial space is shown in the *Henry Percy, Earl of Northumberland* at the Rijksmuseum (Pl. 81), where the various viewpoints introduced in the linear perspective make the foreground ambigious and give the impression that the Earl is not reclining on the grass, but hovering slightly above it; while the blue in the distant landscape is so fierce that it destroys any effect of aerial perspective.

There is none of this confusion in any of Oliver's cabinet miniatures whether the setting is an interior or a landscape; volumes and spatial recession are perfectly realised through the studied use of perspective and composition. His concern for planned composition is evident in the unique pen and ink study for the portrait of '*Lucy Harington*'[93] (Pl. 82). It is not a study for the features, such as those which Holbein had used, but an exploration of the rhythms of the

93. Although it has been suggested on stylistic grounds that this drawing is a copy of the finished miniature by Mathys van den Berg it is so sketchy, and the resemblance of the features to those of the miniature so slight, that it is much more likely that this is a rough compositional sketch by Oliver. A copy would approximate more closely to the finished work in all respects.

composition, and of the pose the sitter was to adopt. In this drawing the features bear little resemblance to the sitter.

Oliver's absolute mastery of human anatomy is not immediately apparent in his miniatures but adds enormously to their feeling of conviction. It is more evident in his drawings, especially the late *Nymphs and Satyrs* (Pl. 83). In the miniatures the figures are normally clothed, although the so-called '*Prodigal Son*' is an exception (Pl. 84). The elaborate costumes generally conceal his knowledge of the forms and articulation of the body. However this can be appreciated in the cabinet miniatures, especially in the *Love Theme*, through the naturalness of the poses and the feeling that the costumes cover real and solid human figures. Why, after writing '. . a hand, or eye by *Hilliard* drawne, is worth an history, By a worse painter made. . .' did John Donne later (1616) sit for Oliver (Pl. 95)? Undoubtably because Dr Donne had discovered an artist who was better at drawing 'a hand, or eye'. It seems likely that Oliver's structural knowledge could only have come from studying anatomical dissection. We cannot know for certain that Oliver attended actual dissections although he could well have had opportunities for they took place at the Universities of Louvain, Paris and Padua. What is fairly evident is that he would have possessed a copy of the 'De Humani Corporis Fabrica' of Vesalius, illustrated with beautiful and explicit engravings derived from drawings by members of Titian's studio, and showing the human figure at various stages of dissection – the first and finest work of its kind. It may be significant that the title page of the first edition included the monogram of its publisher and printer, Johannes Oporinus, in the form of a Greek *phi*; identical with the monogram which Oliver was later to use on his miniatures.

Hilliard's *Young Man among Roses* (Pl. 85) is an anomaly in his *oeuvre*. Quite rightly this miniature has been popularly recognised not only as Hilliard's masterwork, but also as the paradigm of the visual poetry of the Elizabethan age. It is such an enigma in Hilliard's career that its composition may be due to the inspiration of Isaac Oliver.

The *Young Man* was not only Hilliard's first cabinet miniature;

it was also his most masterly and original in conception. It seems incredible that an artist should achieve such a pinnacle of success in a new genre and then steadily descend from one unimaginative composition to another. As Sir Roy Strong has pointed out[94] the miniature leans heavily on the imagery of the mannerism of the Valois court. But there is no evidence of this influence in any other miniature which Hilliard painted after his return from France; yet nearly ten years after his visit he suddenly painted this very studied essay in the French mannerist style. The relaxed and graceful articulation of the figure is immensely superior to any full-length pose which he subsequently painted. Is it pure coincidence that the *Young Man* was painted in about 1587 just about the time of Oliver's association with Hilliard? We know from Oliver's drawing of *The Adoration of the Magi* (Pl. 87) that he was extremely well-versed in the French mannerist style and that he could create original and relaxed composition for cabinet miniatures. The easy *contraposto* of the elongated figure in the entirely new, tall oval shape seems to be closer to the stylishness and compositional daring of Oliver, who in the early *Moses striking the rock* drawing (Pl. 86) allowed the foot of a central figure to overlap the border of the drawing, and later brought novel and exciting rhythms to the old circular limning format in the *so-called Frances Howard* (Pl. 91) and the *Lucy Harington* (Pl. 78).

The unheralded and unrepeated compositional masterpiece of the *Young Man* was therefore most probably inspired by a sketch or suggestion of Oliver's.

Oliver was not a great technical innovator as Hilliard had been. Like Holbein he was content with established miniature techniques and materials, using them selectively and with more deftness to suit his own artistic needs. Every technique of Hilliard's was used by Oliver at one time or another, although the more decorative methods were applied sparingly and were always subject to the spirit of a

---

94. Roy Strong *The Cult of Elizabeth*, 1977. Chapter 2.

particular portrait. His virtuosity and flexibility in handling can best be seen in his modelling of the features over the carnation ground. Unlike Hilliard, who had used the same inflexible and geometrically disciplined hatching in every portrait, Oliver was always capable of suiting his handling to the character of the sitter, or the general feeling of a particular work. This versatility can be seen in the series of early works which are a reaffirmation of the Anglo-Flemish tradition in miniature painting, deserted by Hilliard fifteen years earlier. In these miniatures of the late 1580s Oliver seems to have been extending the new medium to explore its expressive potential and test his own virtuosity. In Oliver's earliest signed work, the small three-quarter length *Unknown woman, aged 20 in 1587* (Pl. 70) the modelling of the minute head is deftly indicated with a few well-placed hatches and stipples. In the following year he painted a series of portraits in which he used different graphic approaches to the delineation of the forms of the features, each of which was adopted to the characterisation of the sitter. In the *Youth, aged 19 in 1588* (Pl. 73) he adopted a vigorous and bold hatching style; this brusqueness was not to be repeated in portrait miniature painting until the mature works of Samuel Cooper in the 1650s and 1660s. In the same year he used a rather querulous hatching line to portray the features of *Diederick Sonoy*; a line which was calculated to give convincing expression to the worried face of the ageing and defeated military commander (Pl. 89). The treatment of the *Unknown Man*, aged 57 in 1588 (Pl. 72) is entirely different. Here Oliver used a very closely wrought stippling to explore the bony structure and the scored and wrinkled features of this old and complacent man. In contrast Oliver painted in 1590 the two *Little Girls aged 5 and 4*, in which he employed a dotted stipple to model the features (Pl. 74). The minute but plump circular blobs of paint serve to emphasise the soft roundness of the childish faces. At about the same time he painted the *Unknown Lady* (Pl. 90) in the Fitzwilliam Museum whose angular features are emphasised by his choice of sharp, parallel hatches to delineate the forms of the head. During the 1590s Oliver's brushwork became less assertive but it rarely ceased to be interesting and creative. He could efface his handling entirely where obtrusive brushwork would have detracted from a miniature's expressiveness; the brushwork of the features was carried out in long straight, fine hatching strokes making Hilliard's hatching appear coarse in comparison. It is unfortunate that in one of the most important works in which Oliver employed this delicate brushwork, the *so-called Frances Howard* (Pl. 91), the flesh-tones have faded, leaving only the soft modelling of the shadows in a grey-brown colour. The gently modelled pink features of this portrait would originally have acted as a subtle foil to the rhythmic composition of silver, grey and black, without detracting from this masterpiece of mannerist design with an ostentatious display of chiaroscuro modelling. The same unobtrusive depiction of the features is evident in the group portrait of the *Brothers Browne* (Pl. 92). In this work the hatching of the features is barely visible, while the handling and colouring of the costumes and the interior is also very restrained. The melancholy figures of the brothers seem to be linked not only physically but by some spiritual empathy and they, and the intruding messenger, are frozen in a dramatic and tragic moment of time. In the *Head of Christ* (Pl. 93), which can be approximately dated as after his trip to Italy in the middle of the 1590s, the head is bathed in a misty light, the *sfumato* effect of which was achieved with soft, close stipples which seem to presage the pointillist manner of the late seventeenth century miniaturist Peter Cross. In contrast Oliver adopted a very linear graphic style in a number of his later works. In male portraits such as the *Sir Richard Leveson* (Pl. 94) this took the form of long vibrant lines and hatches which follow the edges of the planes of the features; while in female portraits, such as the lovely elongated *Anne of Denmark* at Waddesden Manor, the lines are sensitive, almost nervous. In one of his last works, the *Dr Donne* (Pl. 95) at Windsor, Oliver reverted to the vigorous handling of his early *Youth, aged 19 in 1588* (Pl. 73), the firm hatching and stipples strengthening the delineation of the ascetic features of the poet. In most of his late miniatures, however, the features were painted in very smoothly blended hatches and stipples giving the flesh a soft creamy appearance, and it was this manner which Peter Oliver adopted after his father's death. Such handling can be seen in the *Unknown Man*, 1610 (Pl. 96) at the Victoria and Albert Museum; in the series of portraits of *Henry Frederick, Prince of Wales* of which the most important is the rectangular miniature at Windsor (Pl. 99); and in the two portraits of *Richard Sackville, Earl of Dorset* at the V & A (Pl. 79) and the Fitzwilliam Museum. These represent the first appearance of the method extolled by Norgate of adding small amounts of white to the flesh colours, giving them more substance and blending them more subtly into the carnation.

Oliver's other deviations from Hilliard's techniques were few and were prompted by his desire for greater realism. From the beginning he used more opaque heightening in painting the costumes and represented the textures of textiles by their carefully observed folds rather than by relying, as had Hilliard, on the texture of his pigments. He avoided the burnished gold inscriptions favoured by Hilliard quite early in his career, probably because these detracted from the realism to which he was dedicated. When he did use gold it was often unburnished and sometimes he reverted to the pre-Hilliard method of painting the gold edge-line quite thinly over the vellum.

Unlike Hilliard, Oliver left a powerful artistic legacy to the limners of the seventeenth century. Some thirty years after his death his most talented successor, Samuel Cooper, was building on the originality and freedom of execution of Oliver's works to produce miniatures which were not merely an imitation of Van Dyck's Baroque style but a direct challenge to the Baroque easel portrait. Cooper had been subjected to the powerful influence of Isaac Oliver through two metropolitan studios which had inherited his style and techniques. While Lawrence Hilliard had been struggling ineffectually to come to terms with the new demand for realism, Peter Oliver had perfected these aspects of his father's late style which became crucial to the development of the miniature throughout the seventeenth century. By 1630 John Hoskins was working in a manner which was derived from Isaac Oliver through the influence of his son. Comparing Hoskins' ambitious cabinet miniature of *Lady Dysart* at Ham House (Pl. 97) with Isaac Oliver's rectangular miniature of *Henry Frederick, Prince of Wales* at Windsor (Pl. 99) emphasises Hoskins' debt. The features of Lady Dysart are modelled in that same blended style resulting from the addition of white to the flesh colours; the costume is modelled realistically with gouache and the landscape and figure are integrated with a naturalism deeply reminiscent of Oliver.

Samuel Cooper was trained in this tradition by John Hoskins, his uncle. Isaac would certainly have approved of the young artist's original development of inherited techniques to create yet another renaissance of the English miniature.

THE PLATES

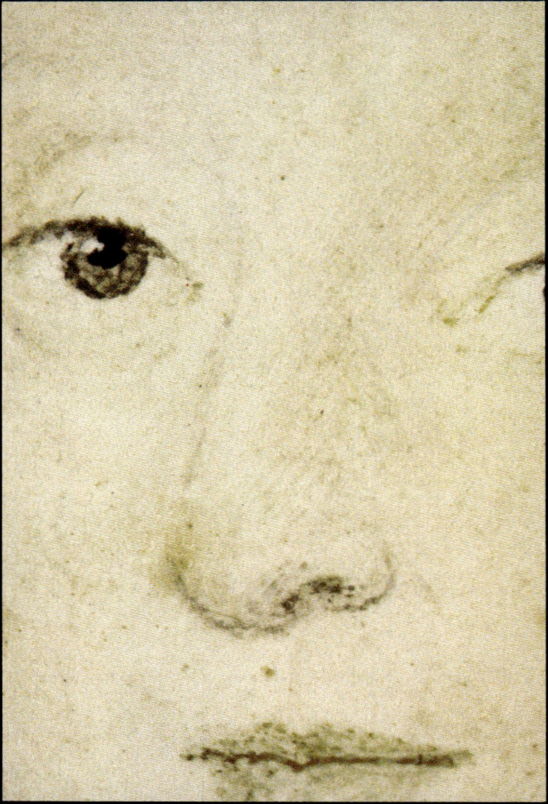

A

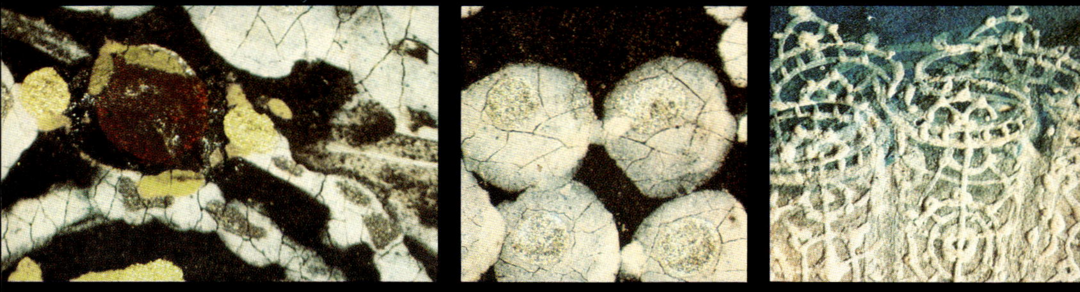

B C D

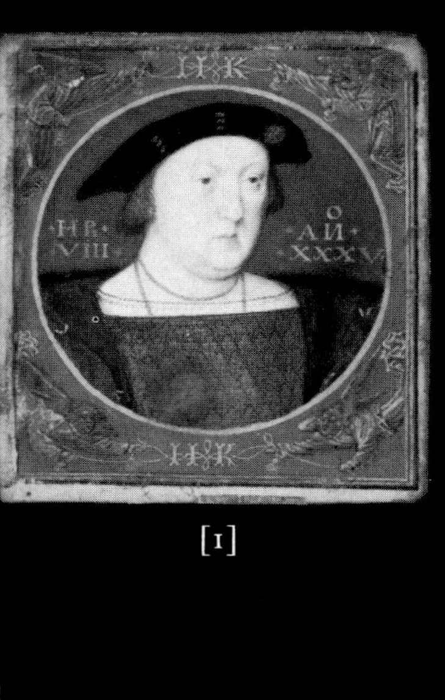
HR VIII
AN XXXV

[1]

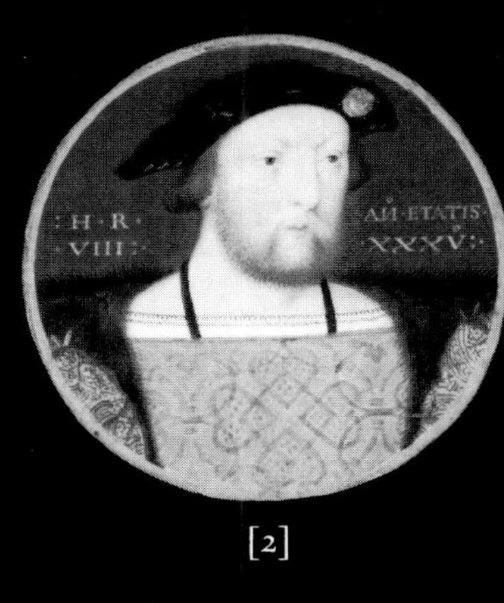
H · R · VIII
AN ETATIS XXXV

[2]

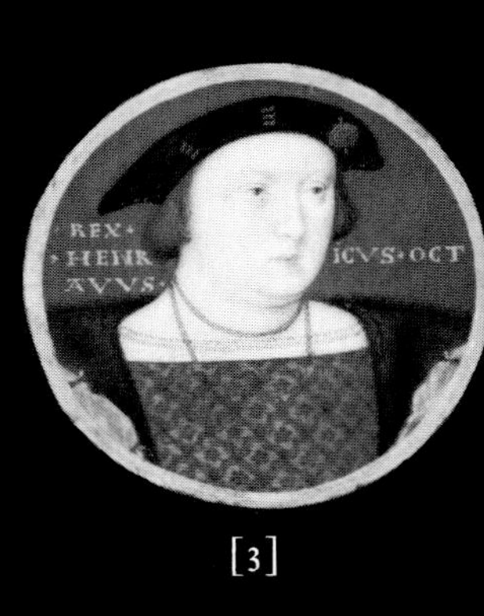
REX HENR ICVS OCT AVVS

[3]

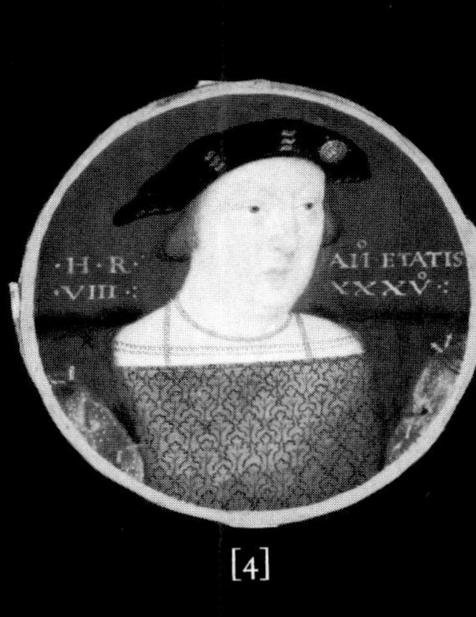
H · R · VIII
AN ETATIS XXXV

[4]

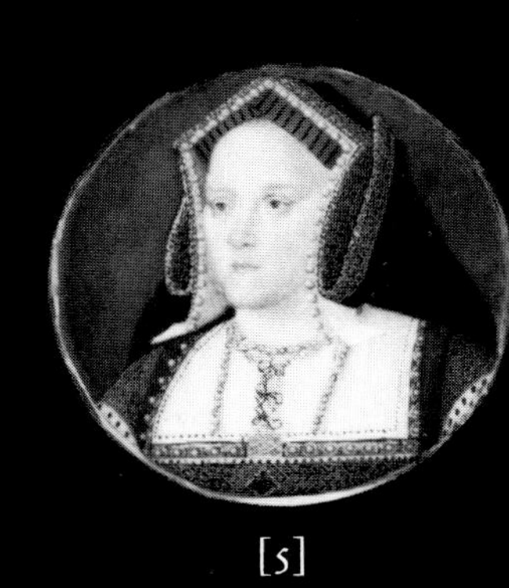

[5]

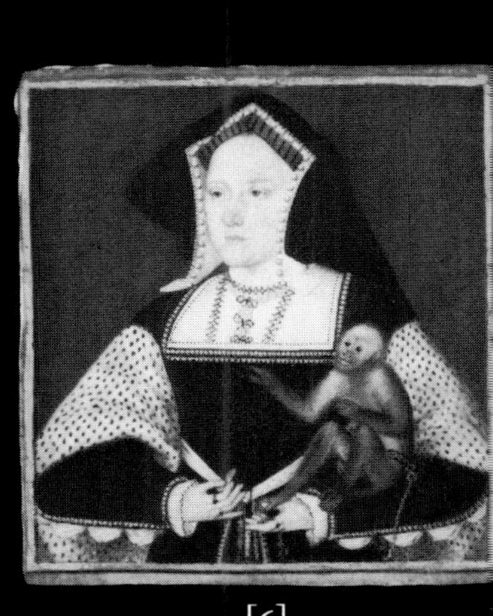

[6]

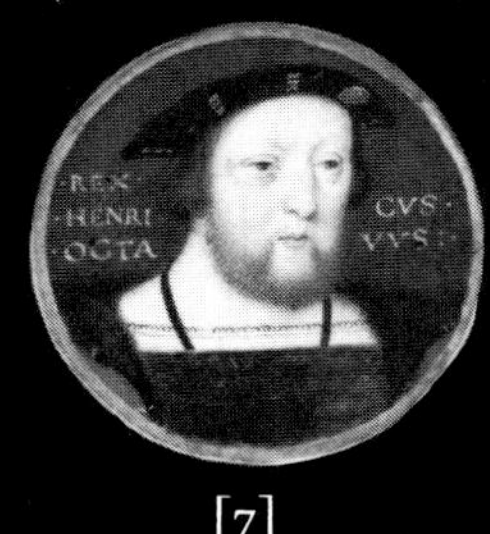
REX
HENRI
OCTA
CVS
VVS

[7]

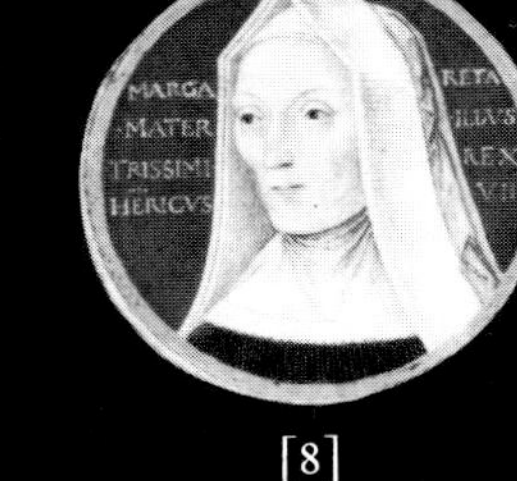
MARGA
MATER
TRISSIMI
HERICVS
RETA
ILLVS
REX
VII

[8]

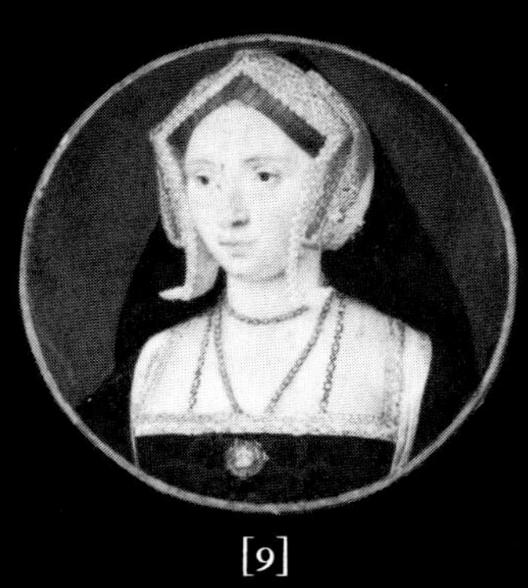

[9]

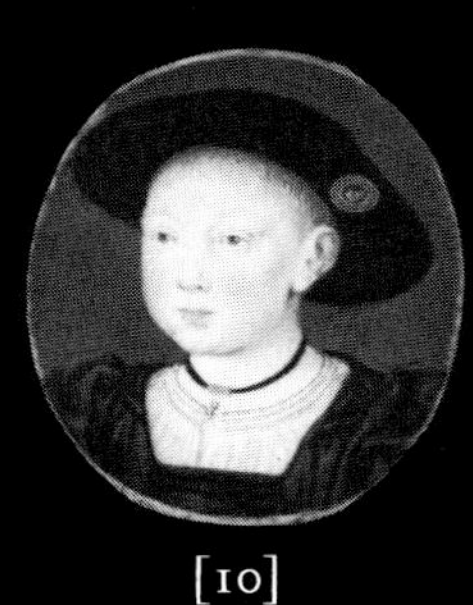

[10]

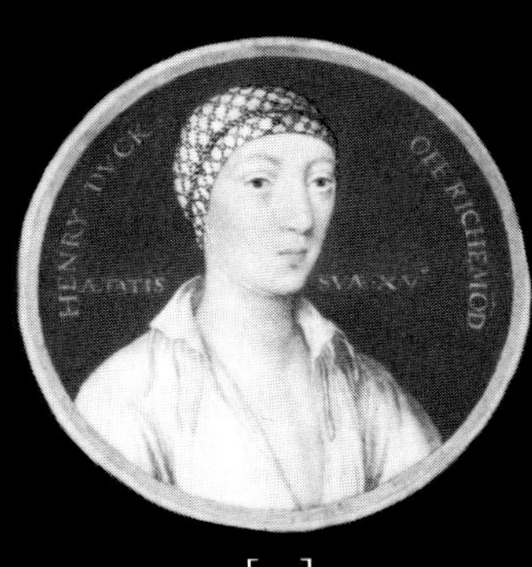
HENRY DVCK
OFF RICHEMOD
ÆTATIS
SVÆ XV

[11]

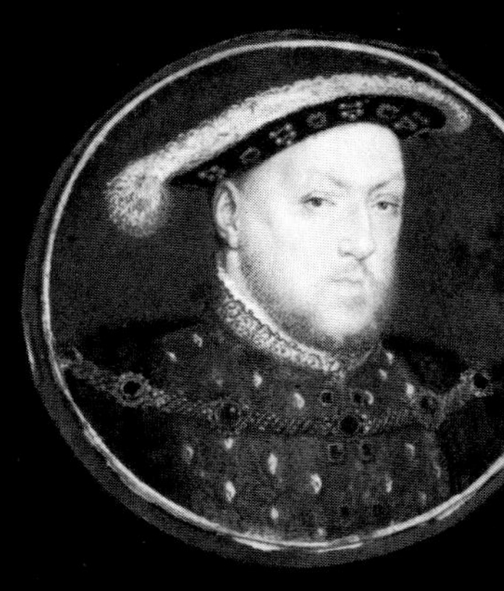

[12]

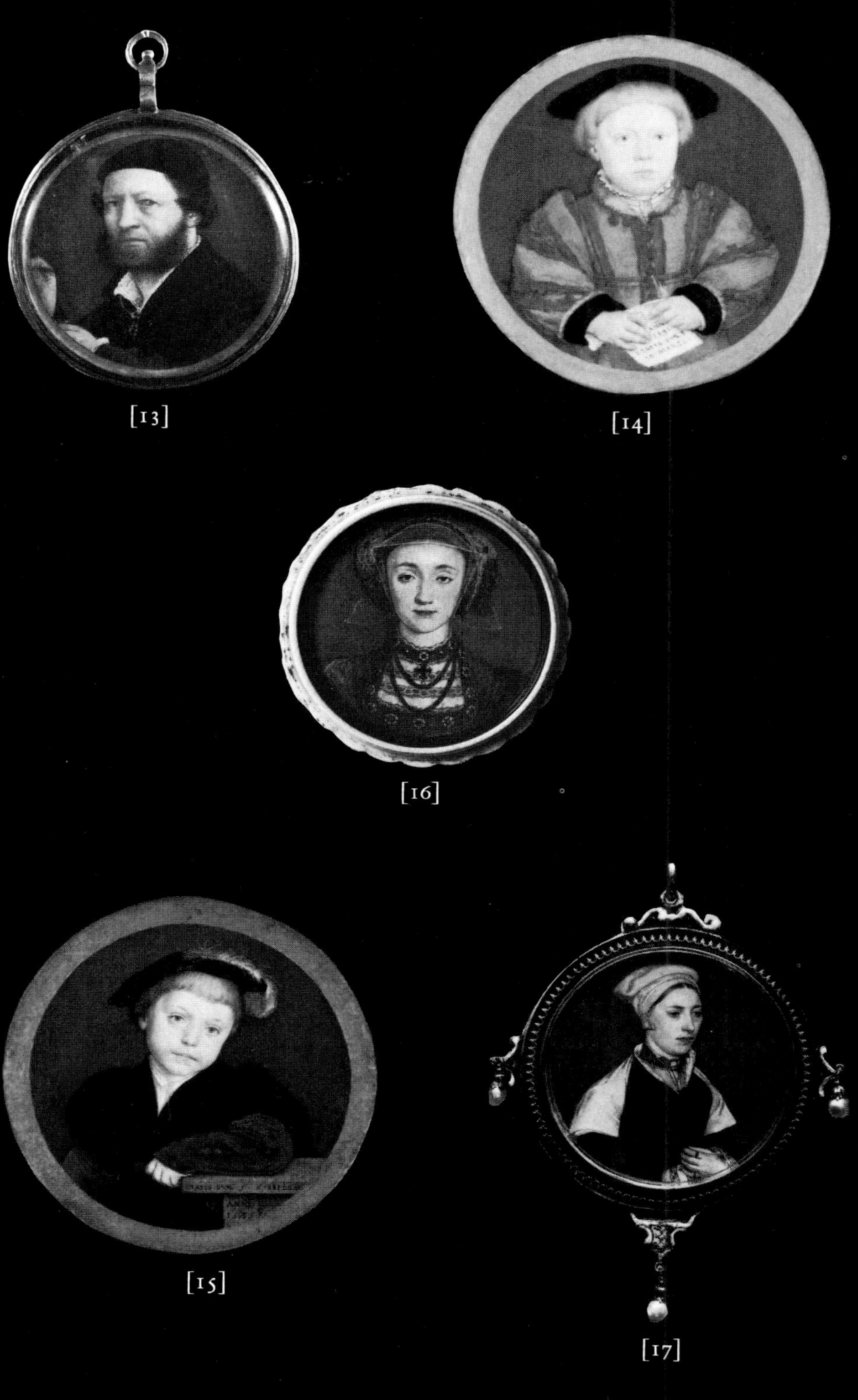

[13]

[14]

[16]

[15]

[17]

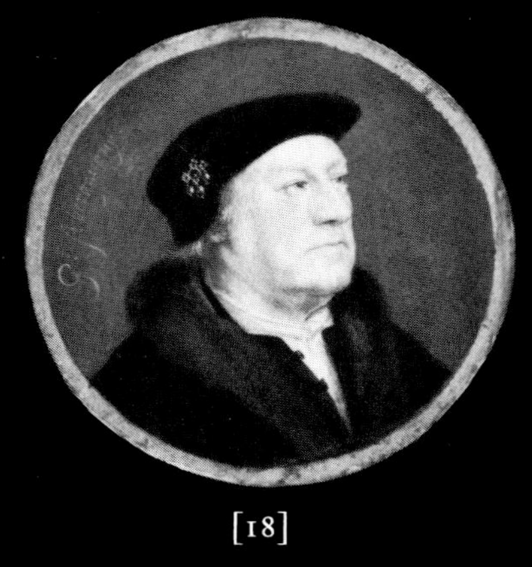

[18]

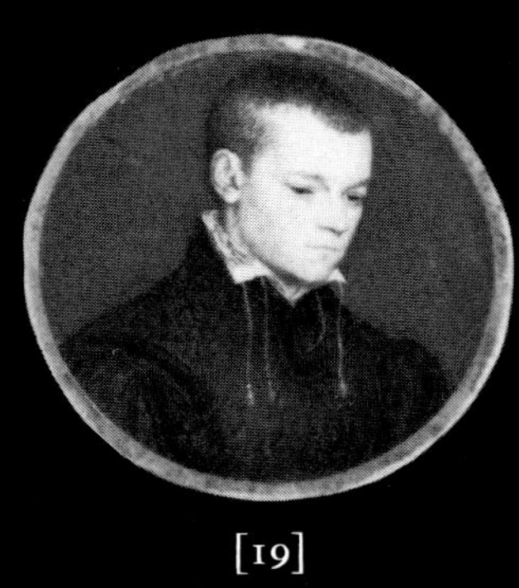

[19]

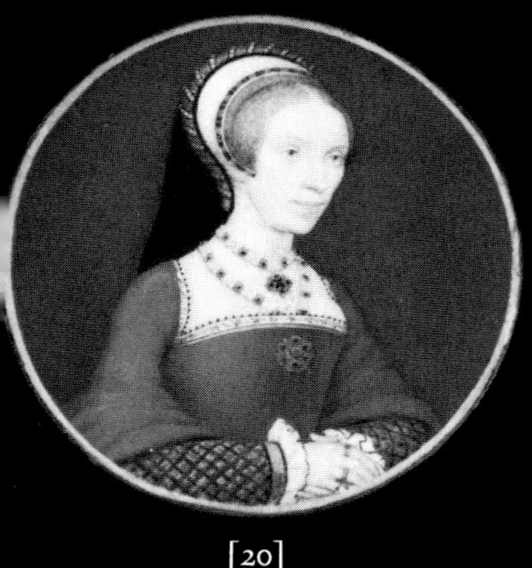

[20]

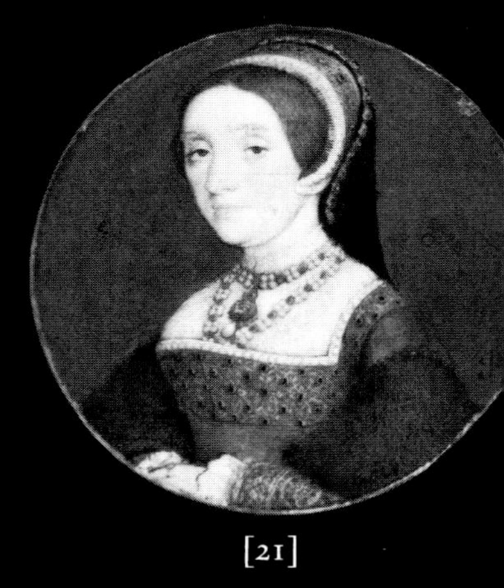

[21]

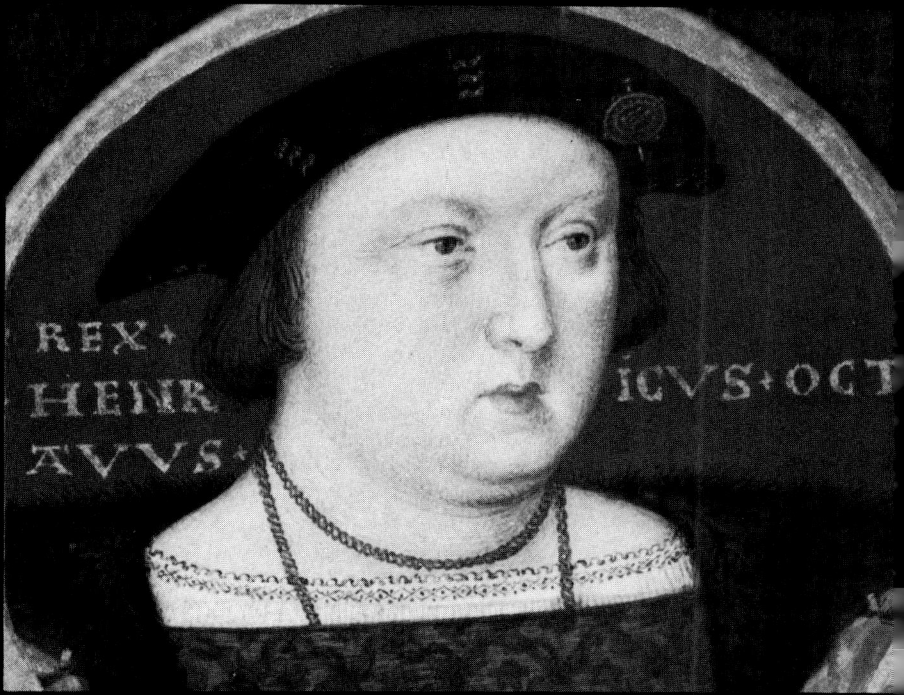

[22]

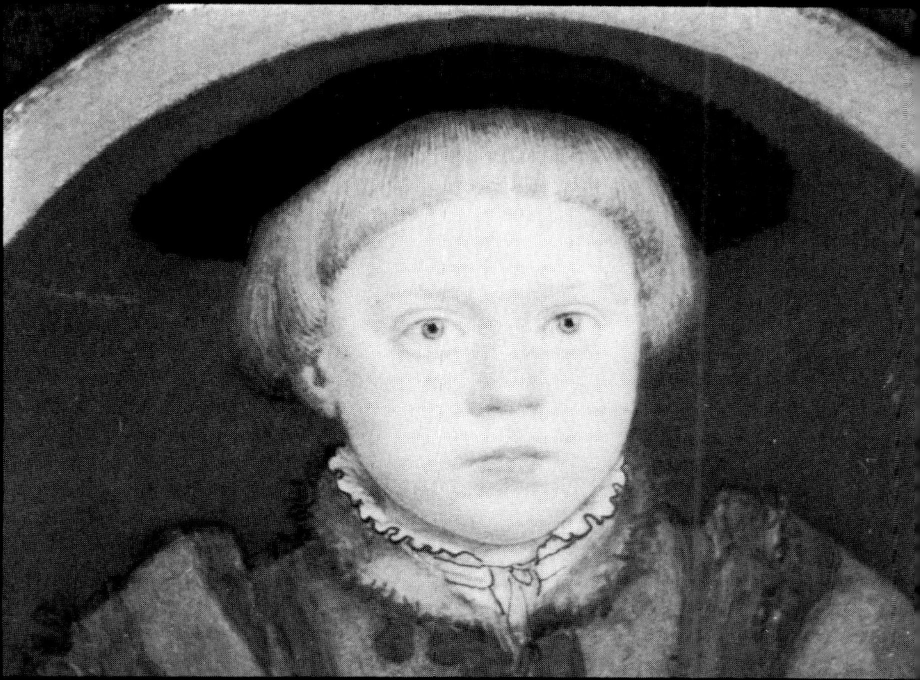

[23]

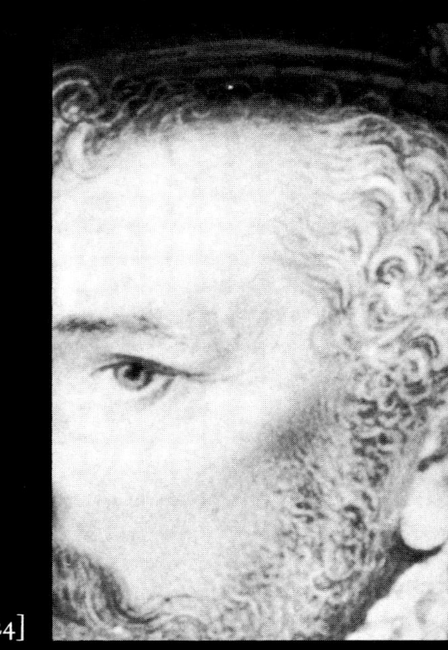

[24]

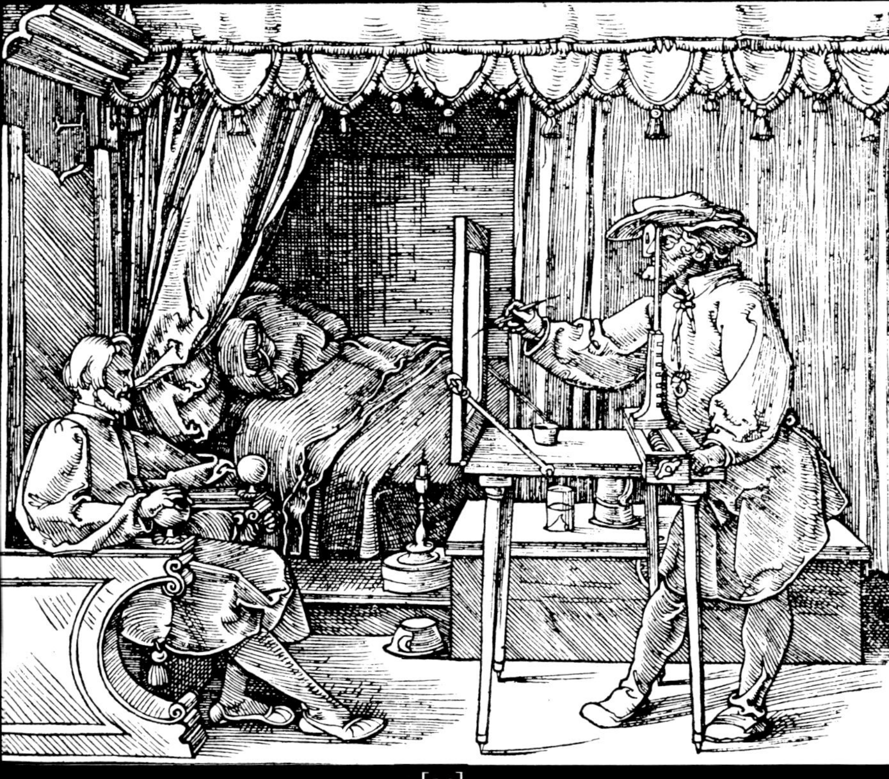

[25]

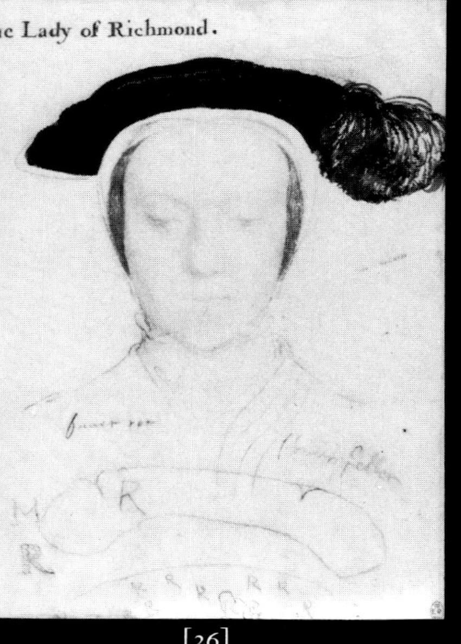
he Lady of Richmond.

[26]

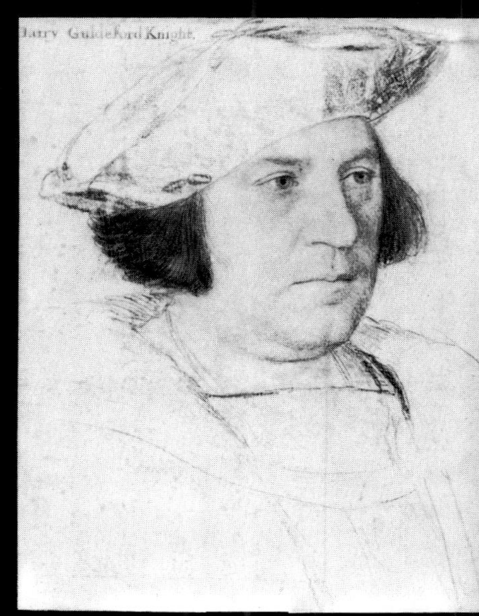
Harry Guldeford Knight.

[27]

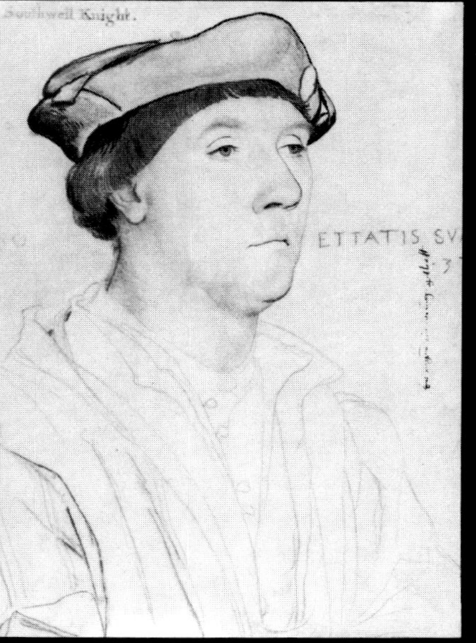
Southwell Knight.
ETTATIS SV

[28]

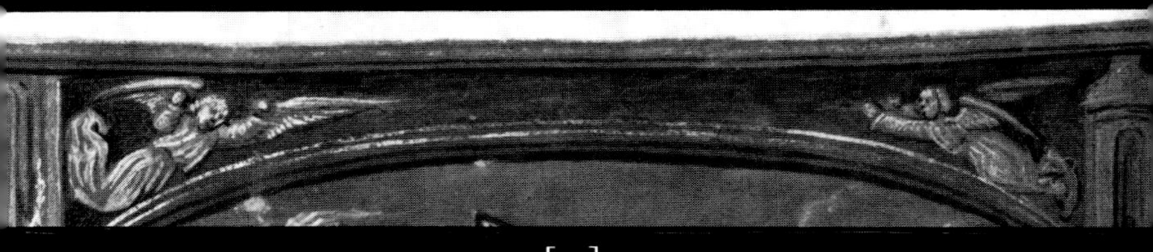

[29]

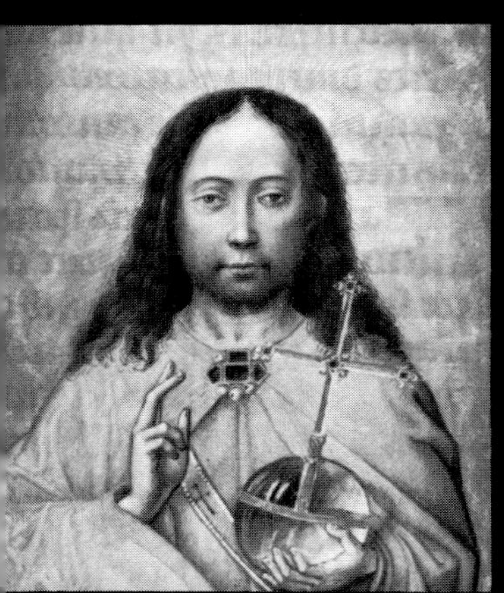

[30]

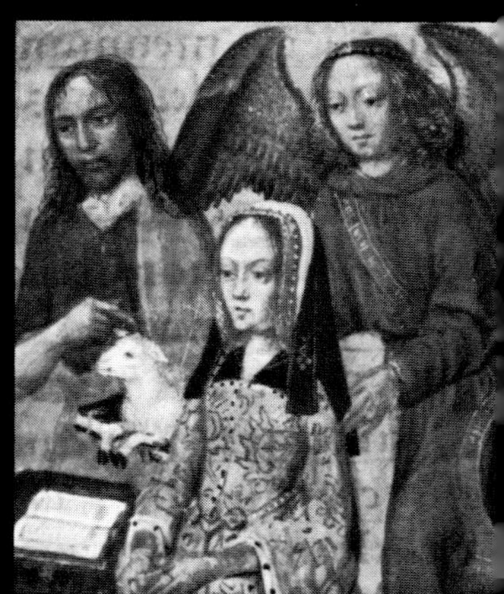

[31]

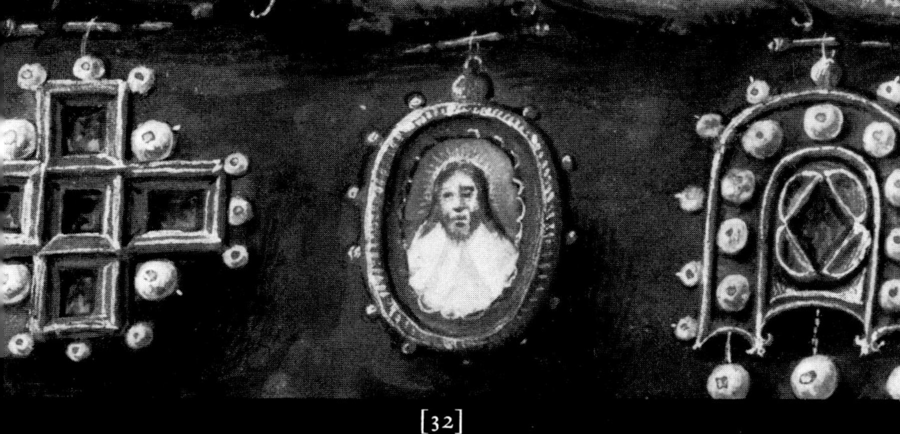

[32]

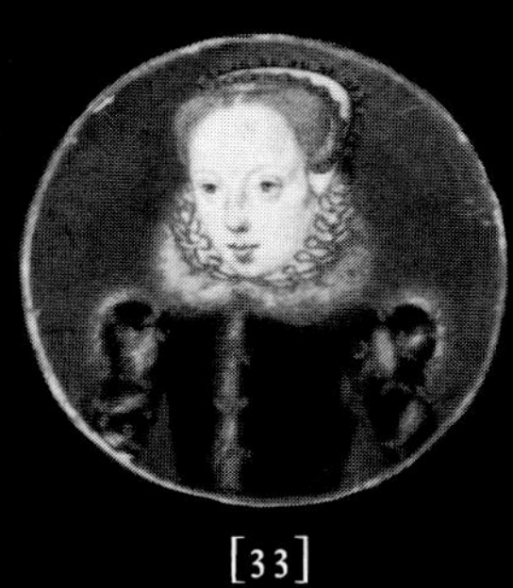

[33]

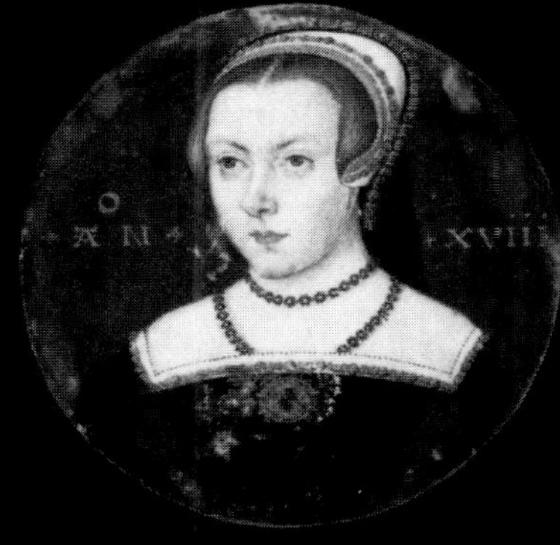

[34]

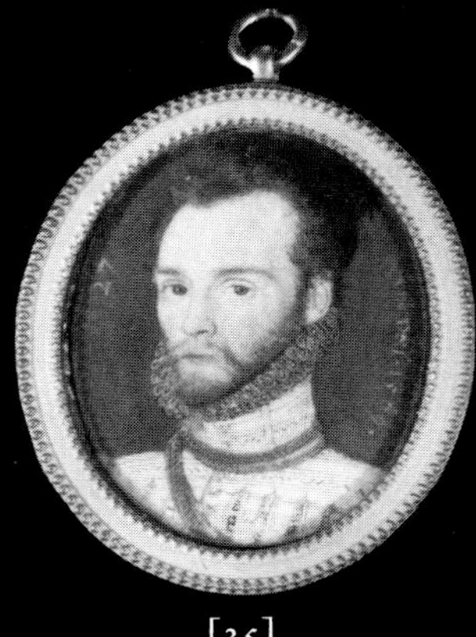

[35]

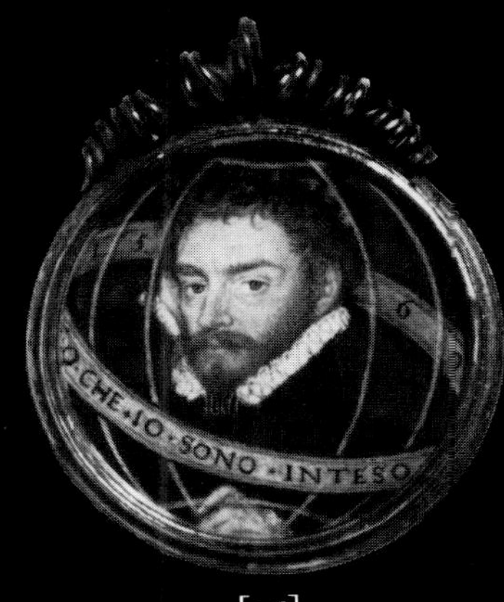

[36]

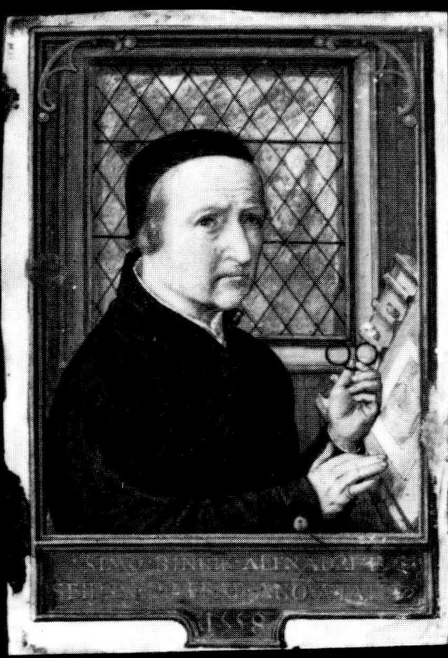

[37]

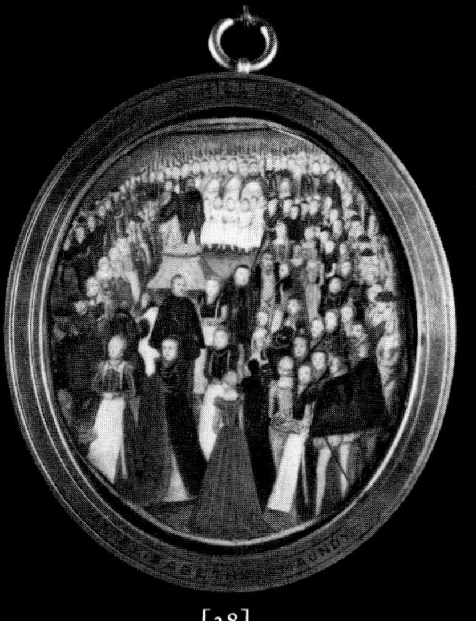

[38]

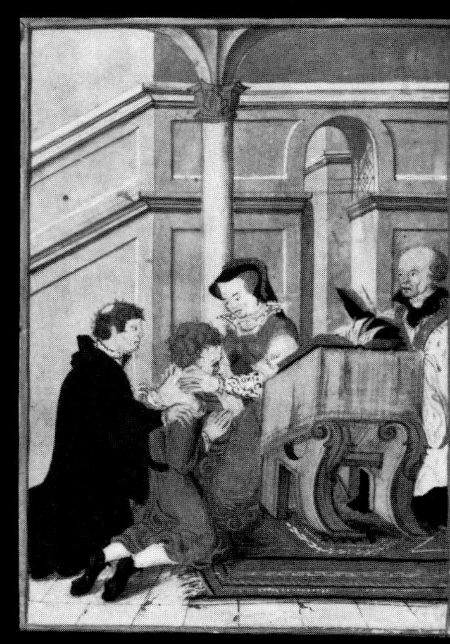

[39]

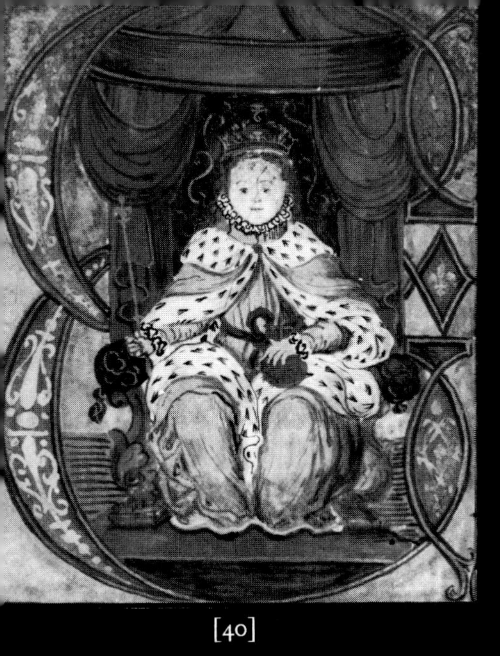

[40]

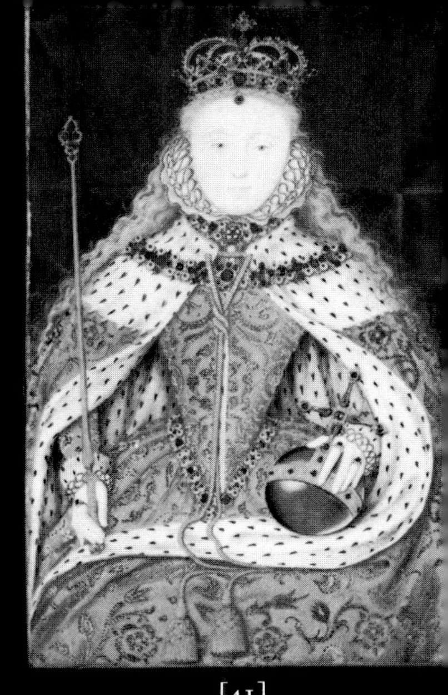

[41]

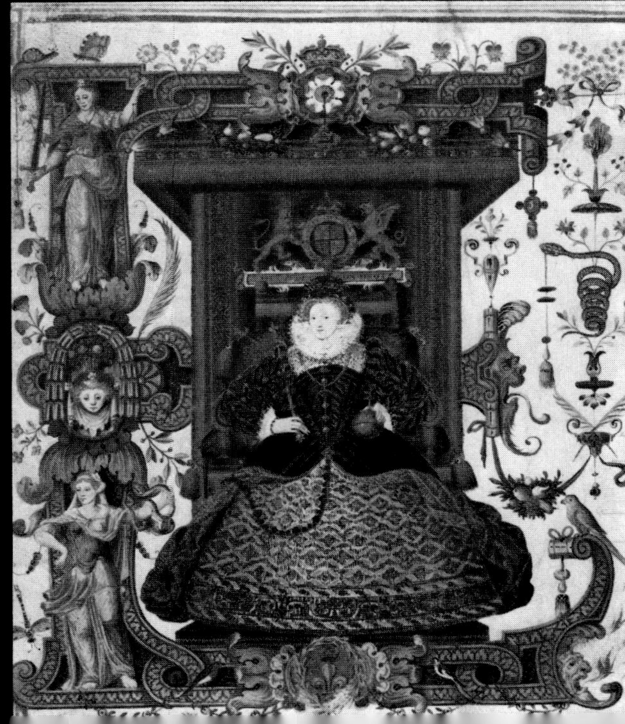

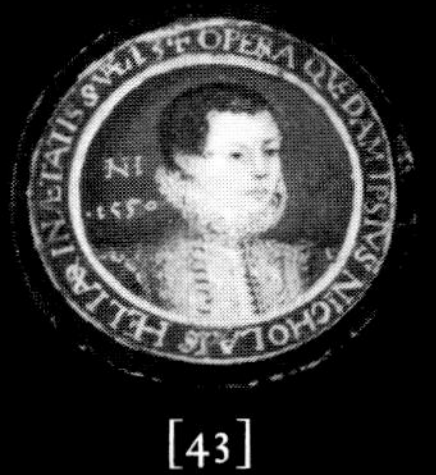

[43]

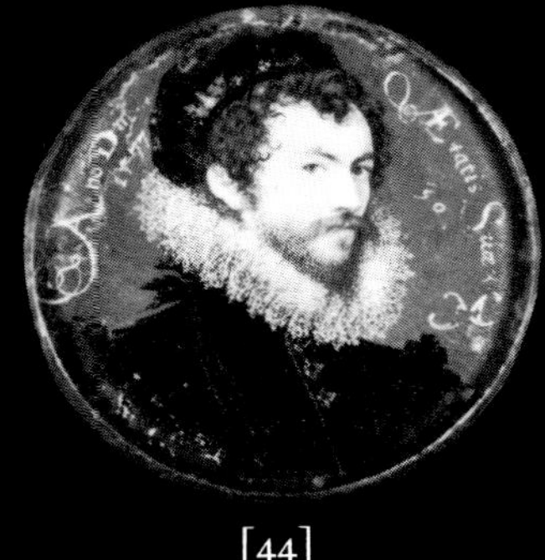

[44]

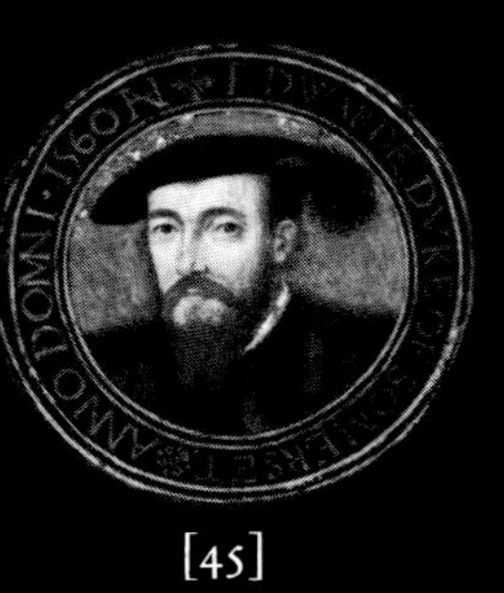

[45]

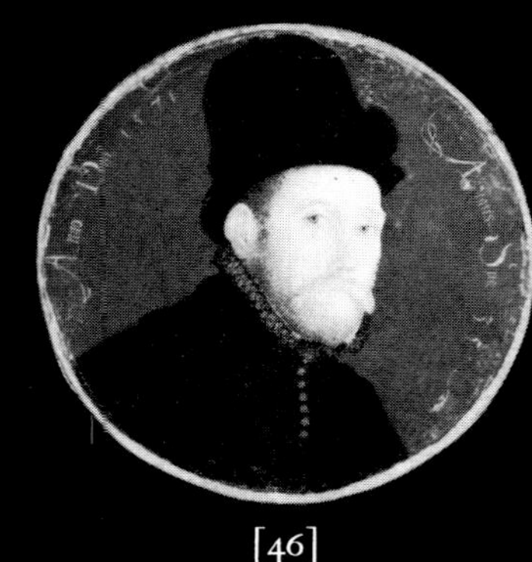

[46]

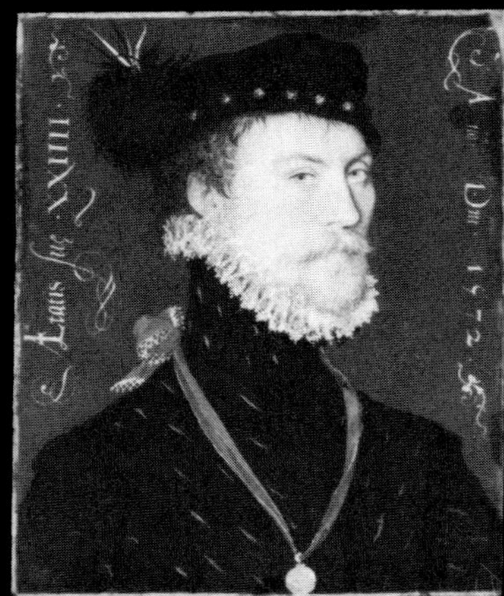

[47]

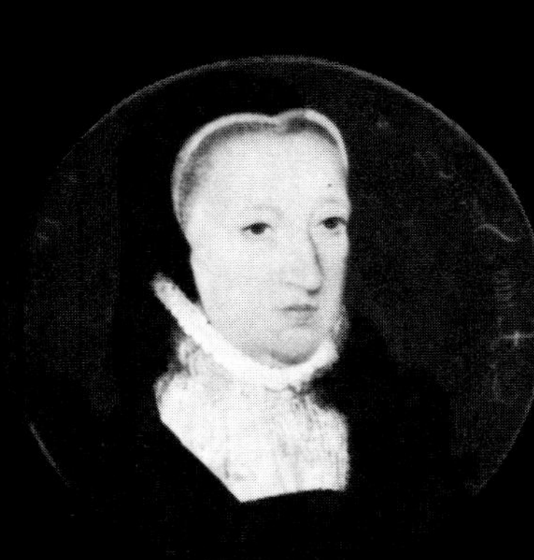

[48]

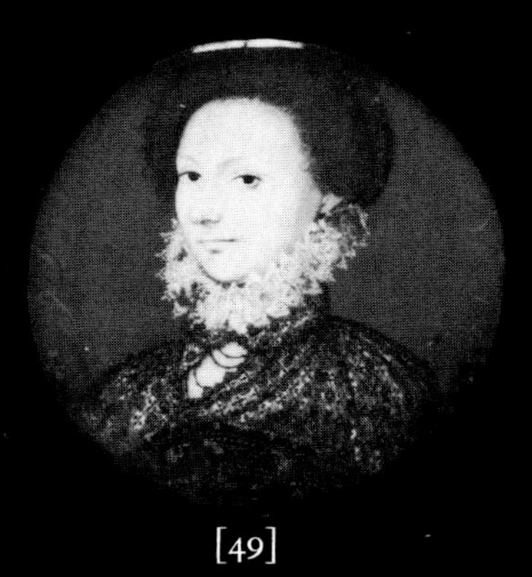
[49]

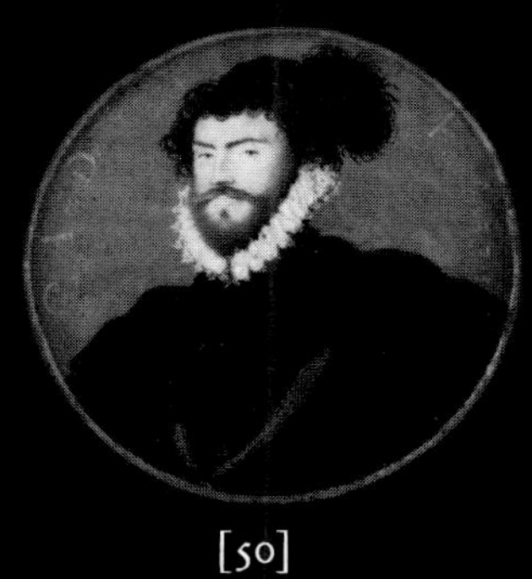
[50]

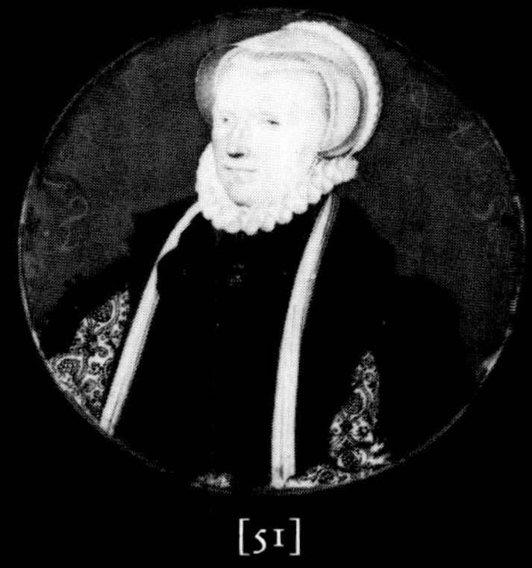
[51]

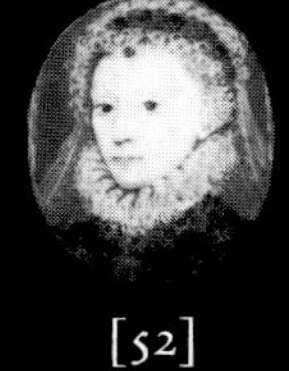
[52]

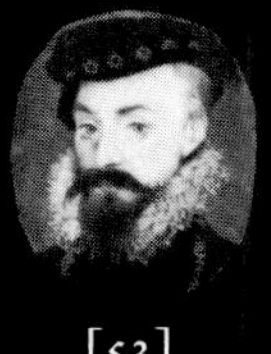
[53]

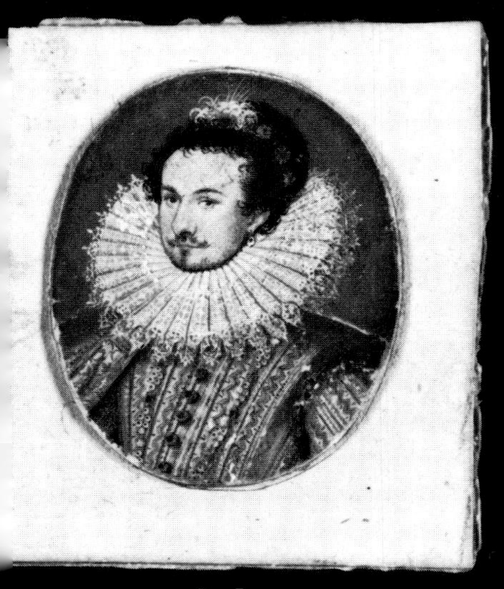

[54]

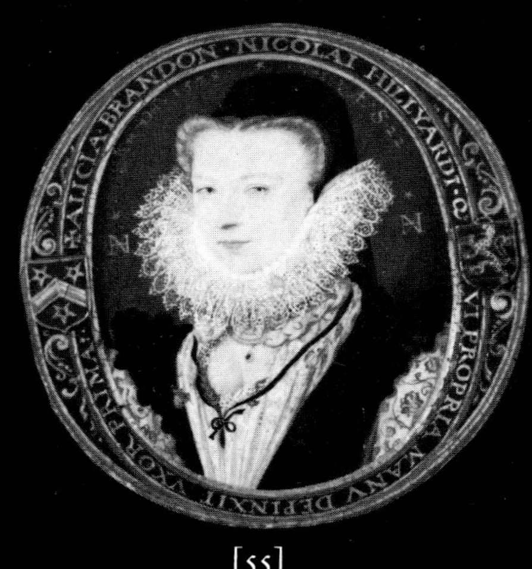
ALICIA·BRANDON·NICOLAI HILLYARDI·
VI PROPRIA MANV DEPINXIT VXOR PRIMA

[55]

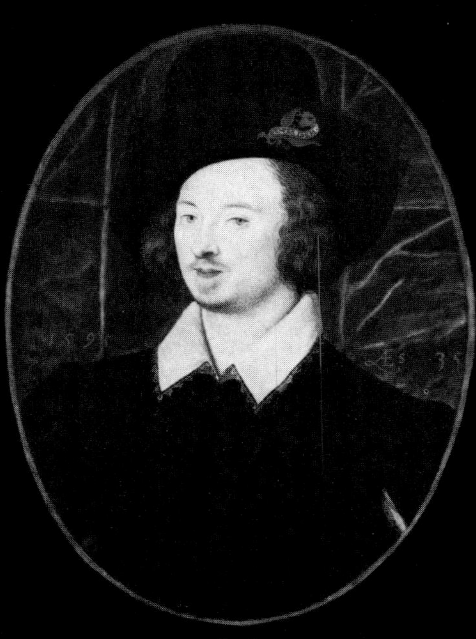

[56]

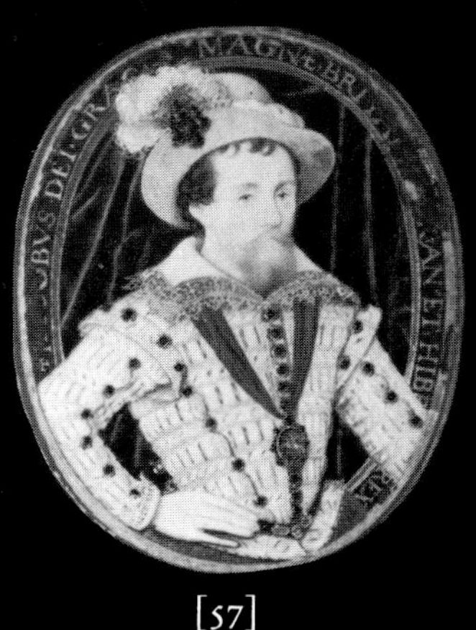

[57]

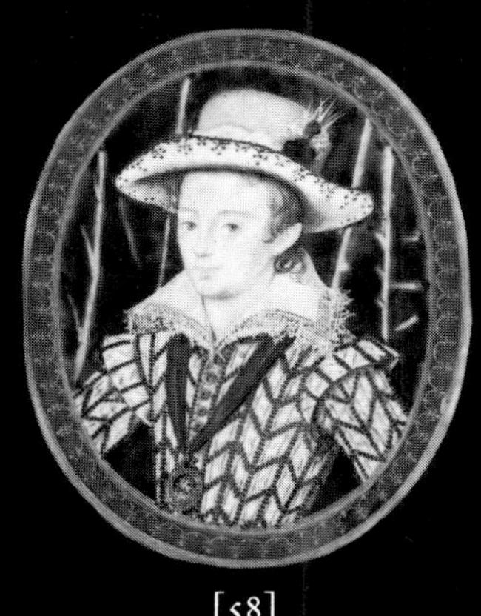

[58]

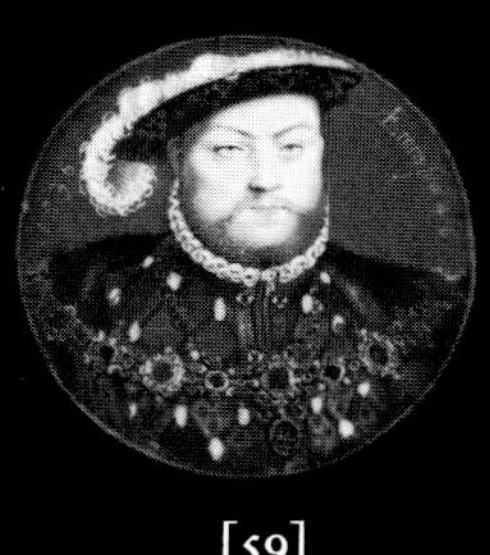

[59]

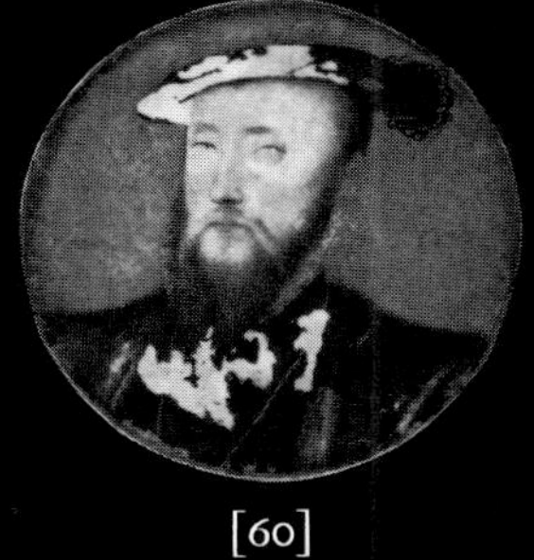

[60]

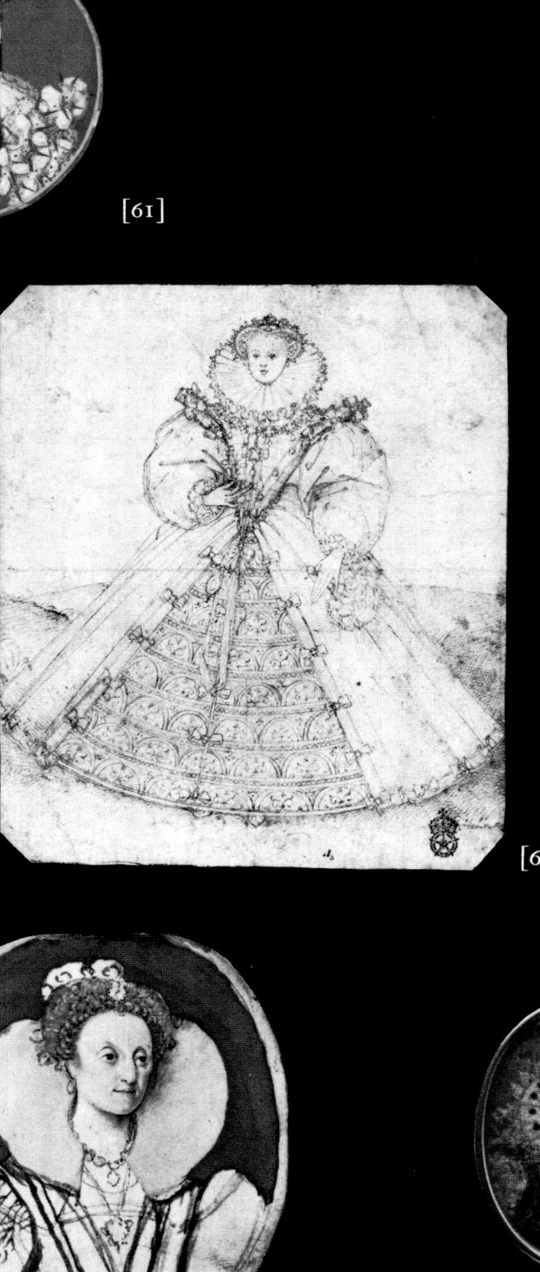

[61]

[62]

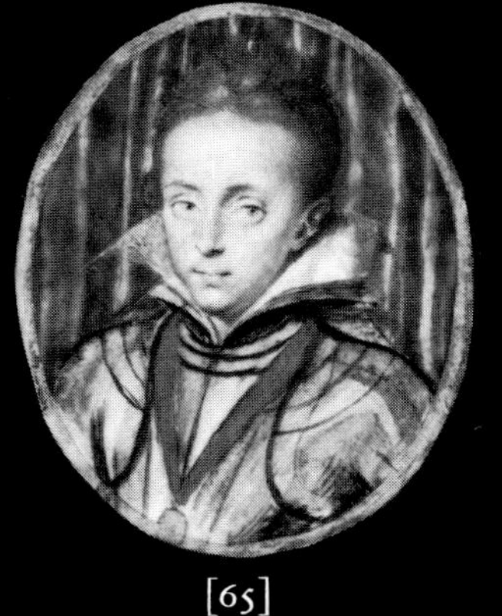

[65]

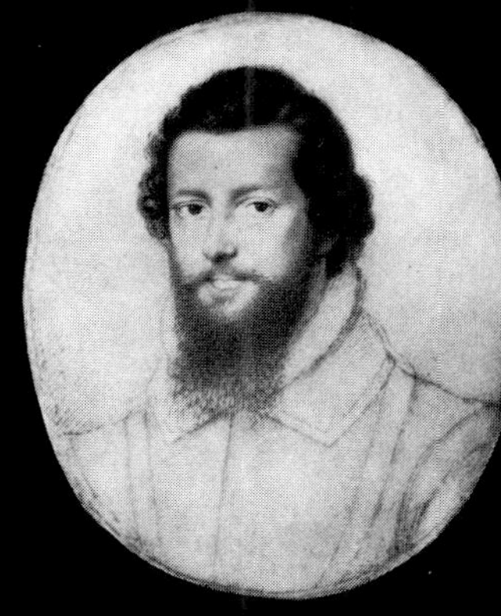

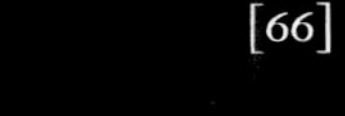

[66]

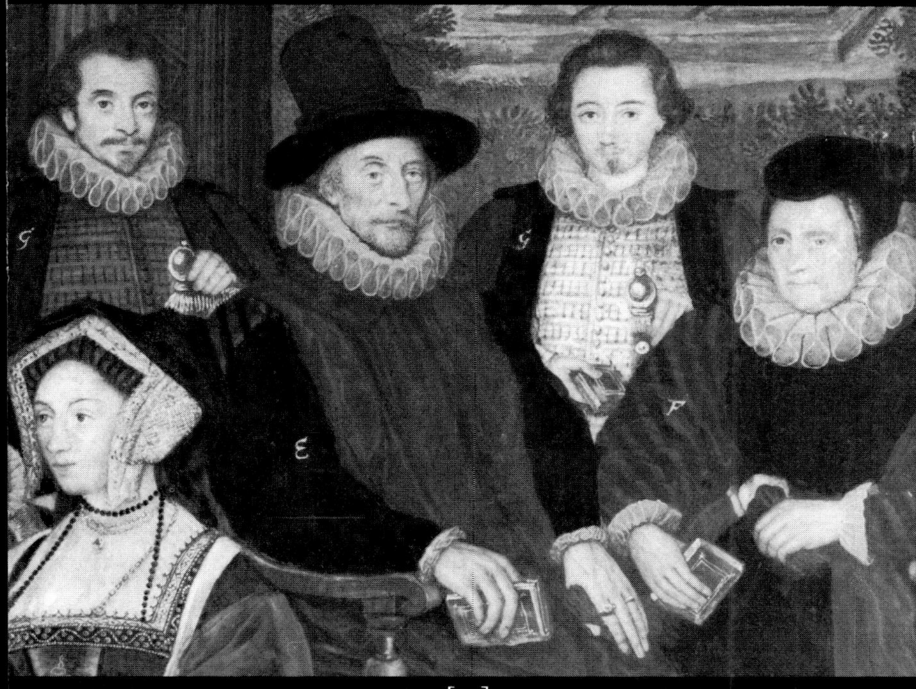

[67]

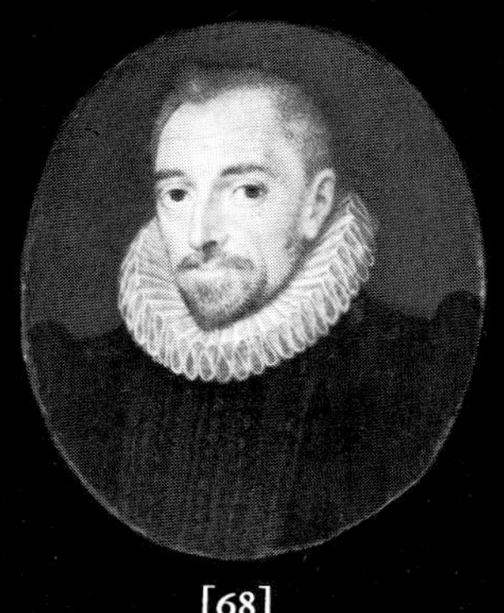

[68]

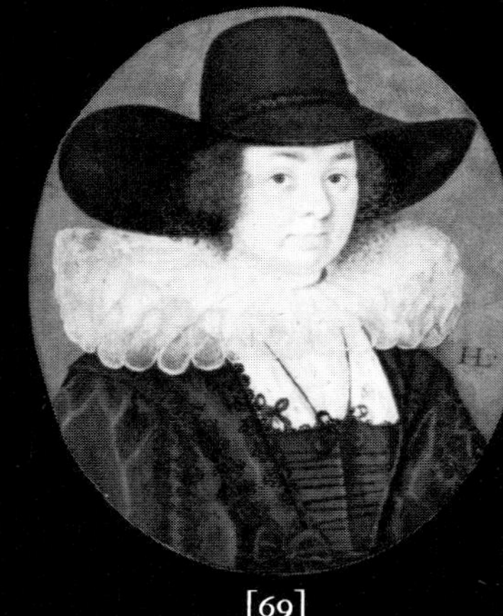

[69]

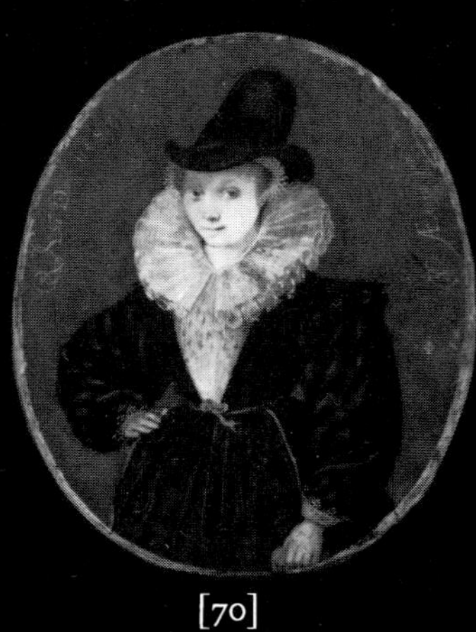

[70]

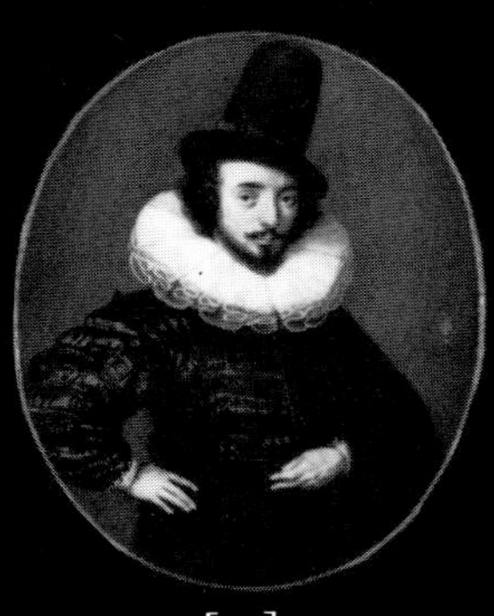

[71]

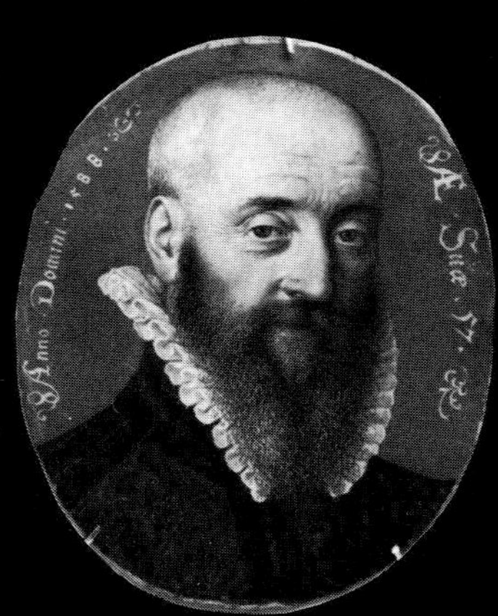

[72]

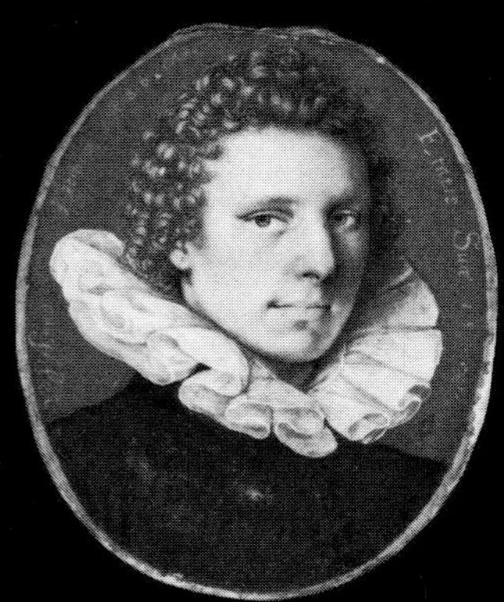

[73]

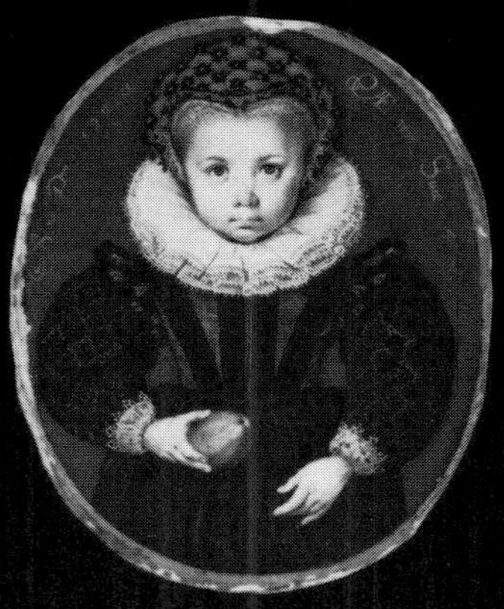

[74]

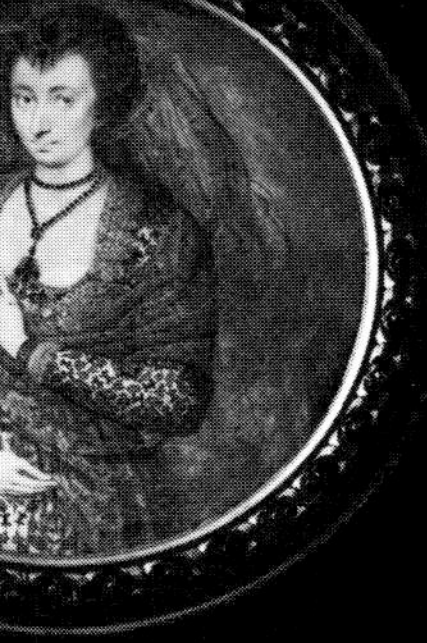

[78]

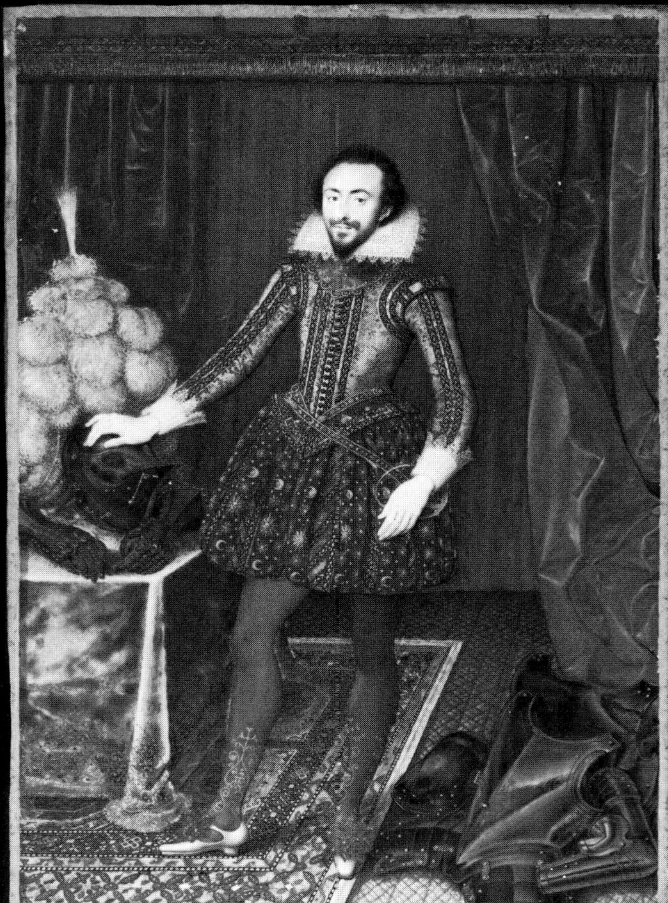

[79]

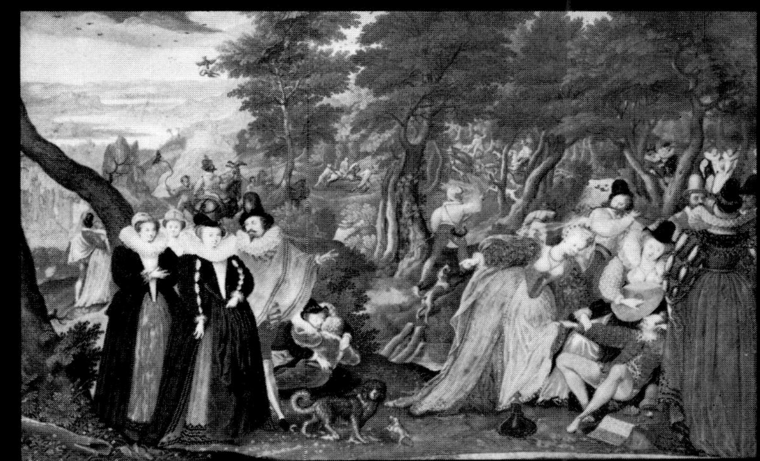

[80]

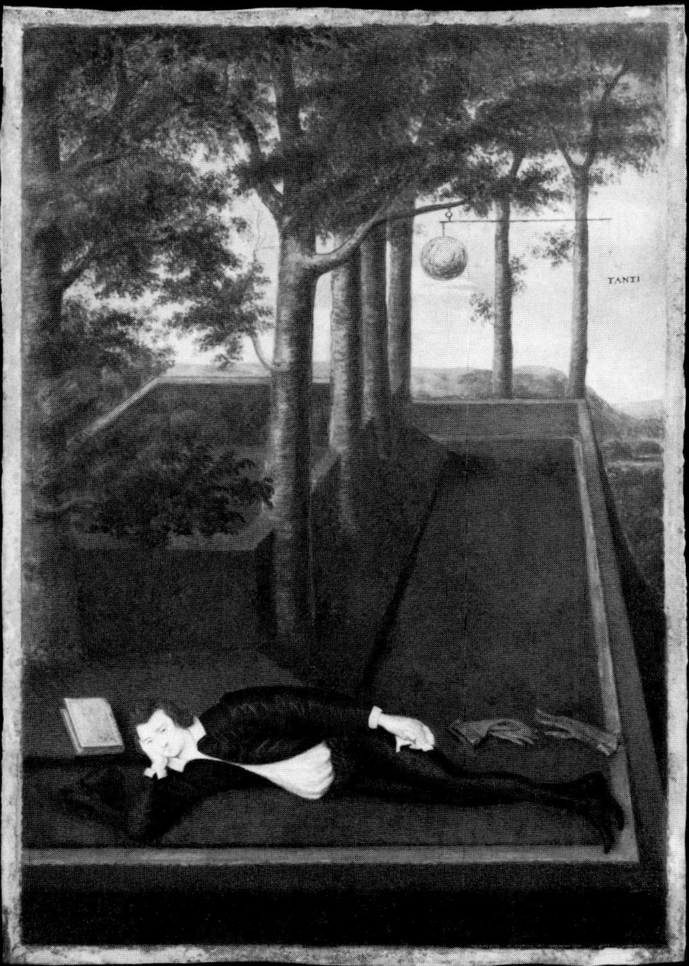

TANTI

[81]

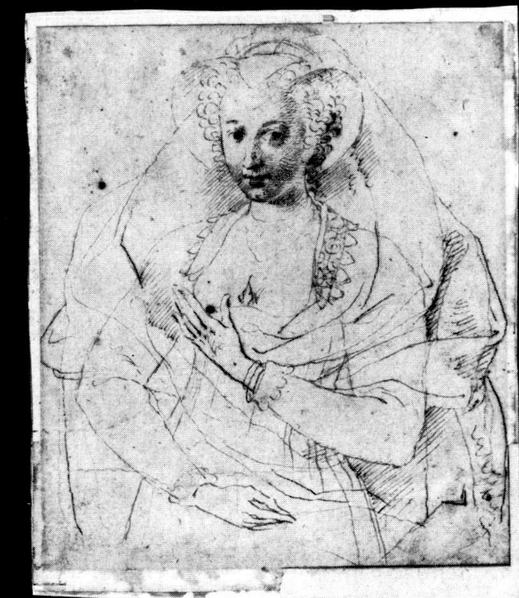

[82]

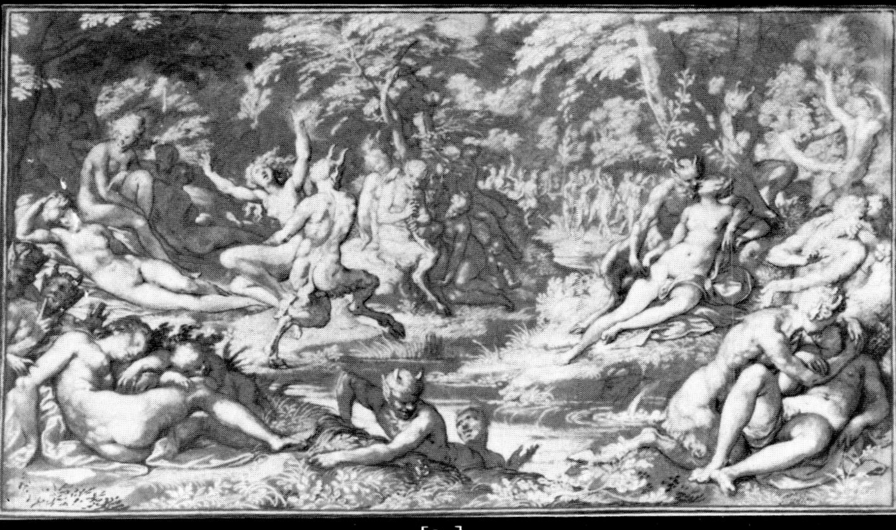

[83]

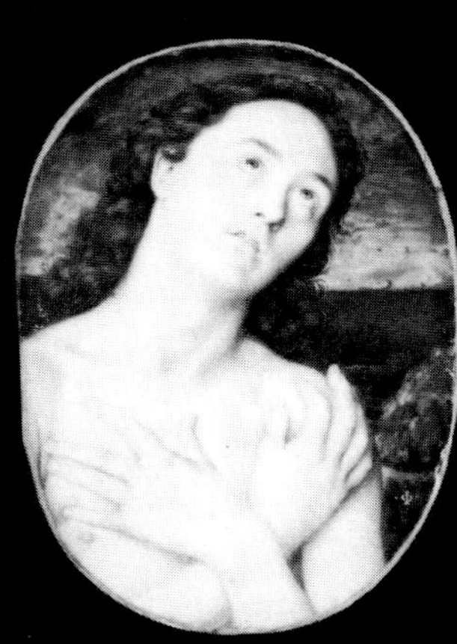

[84]

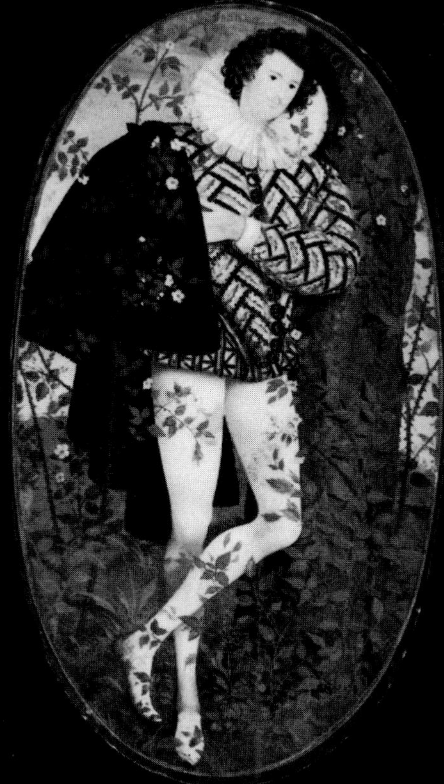

[85]

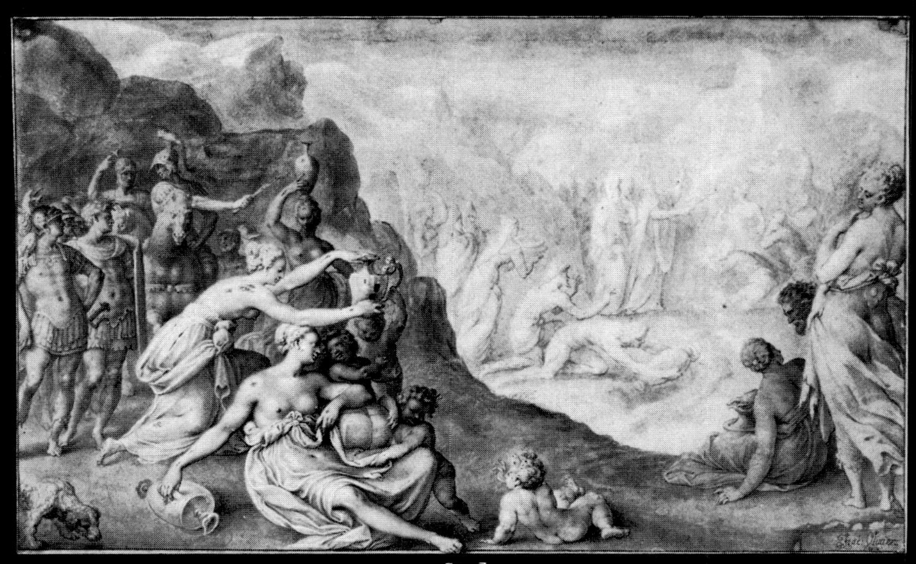

[86]

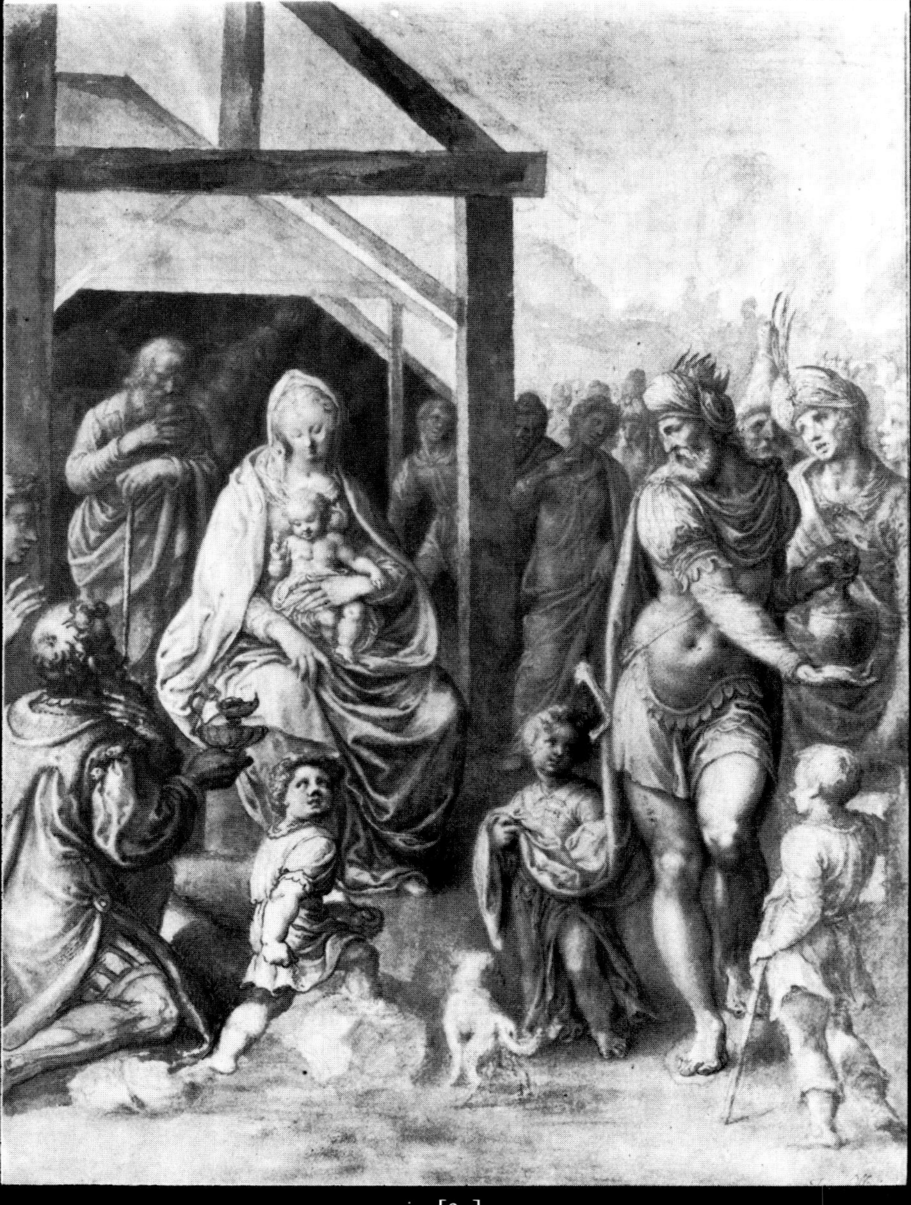

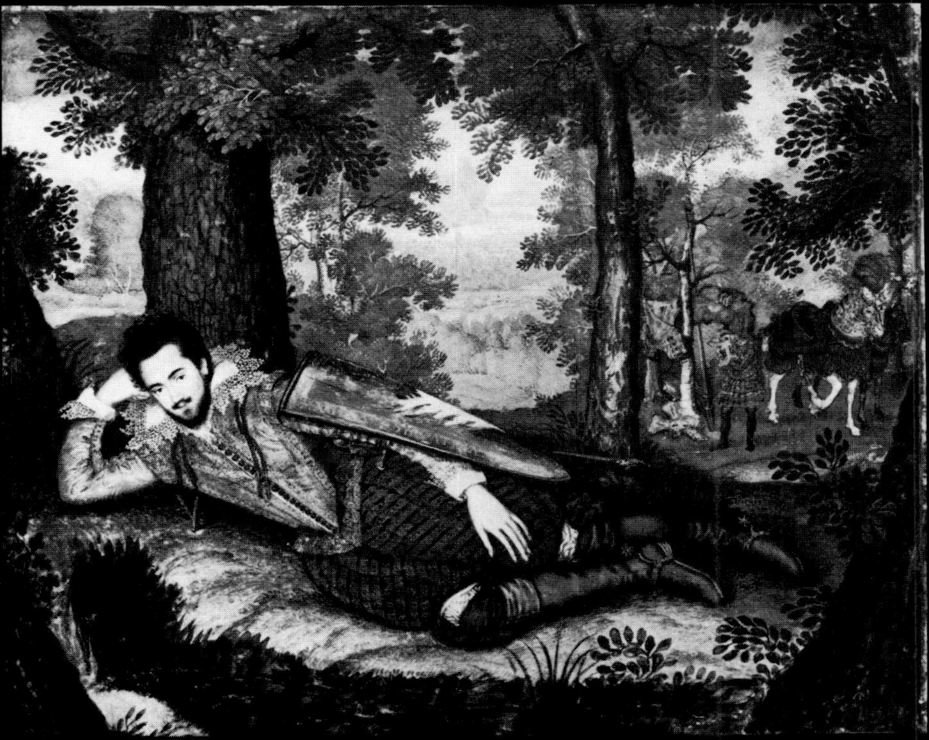

[88]

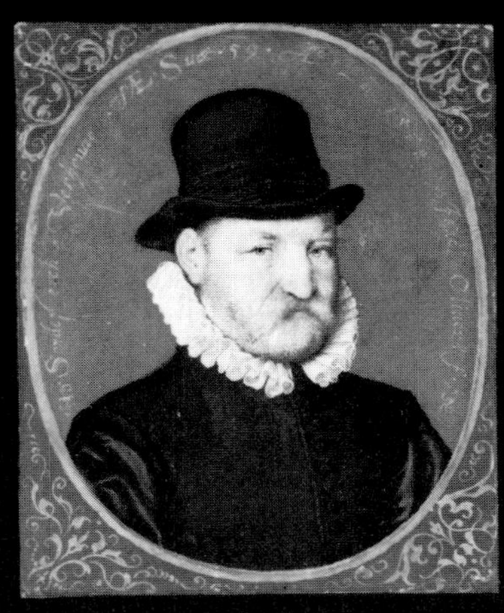

[89]

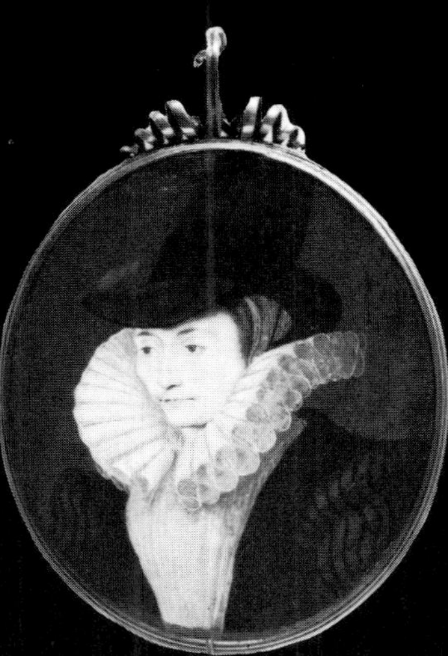

[90]

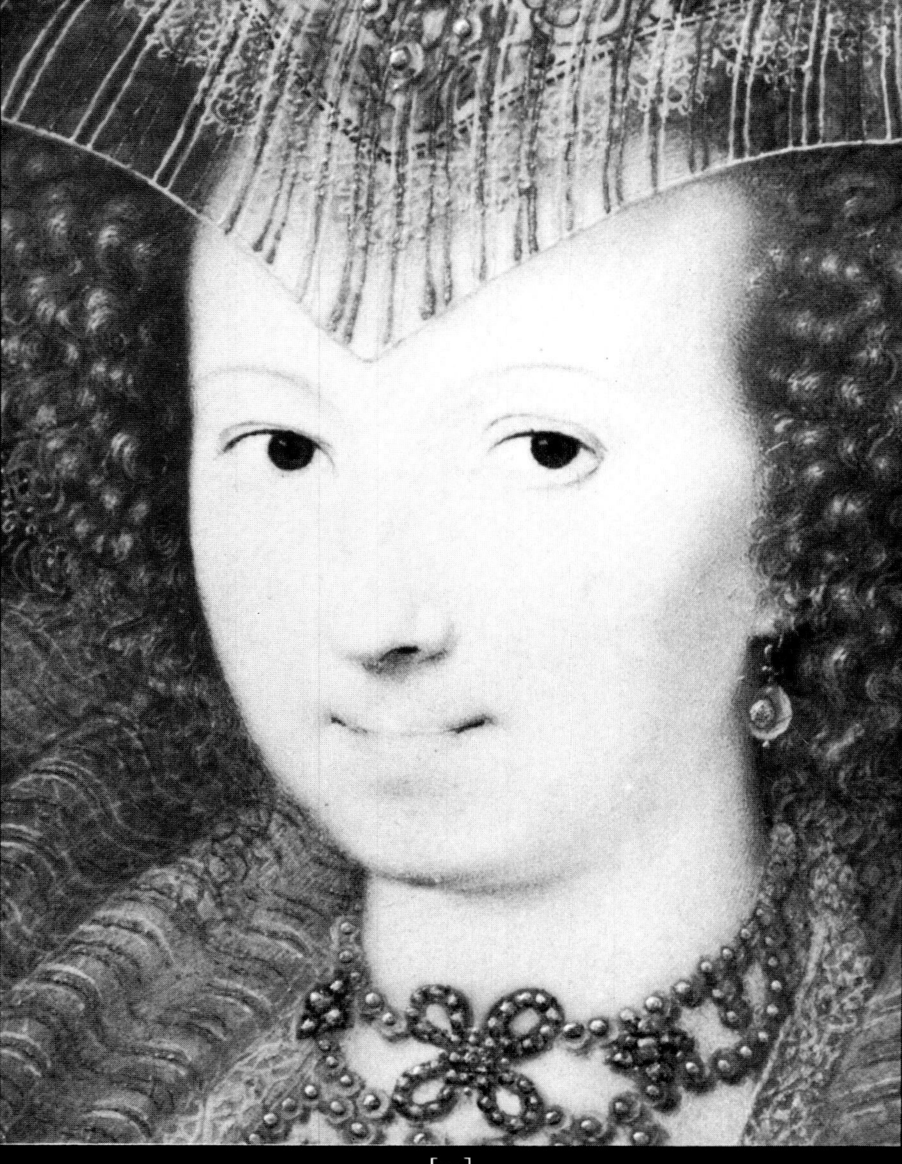

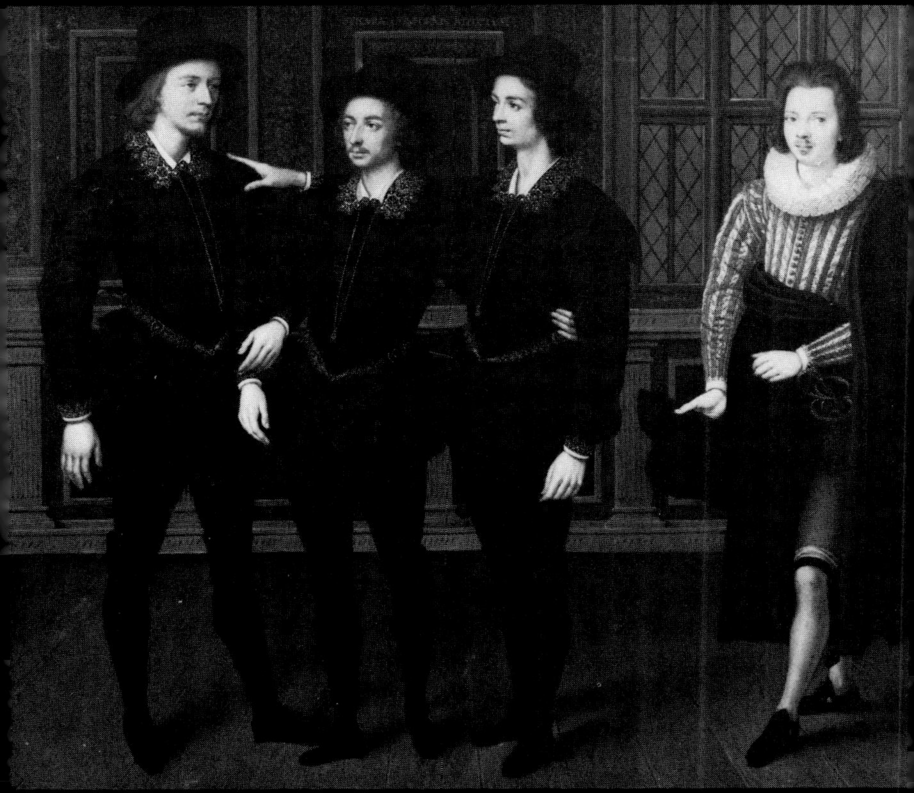

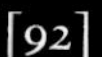

[92]

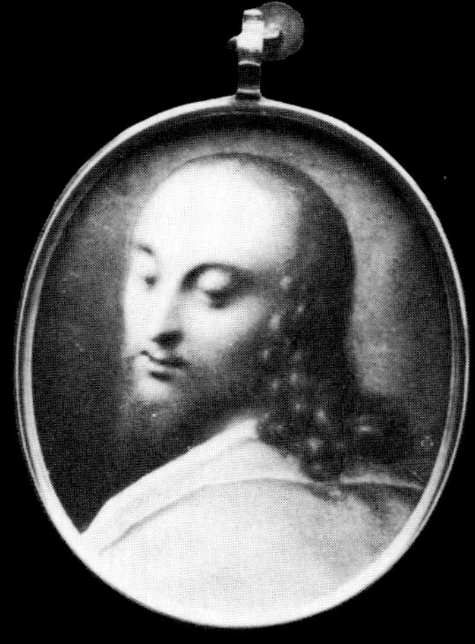

[93]

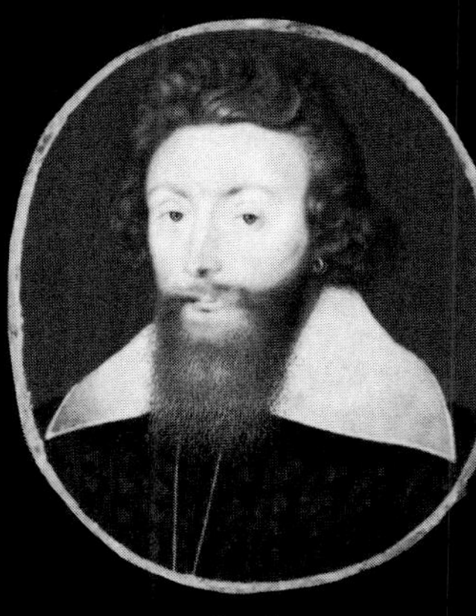

[94]

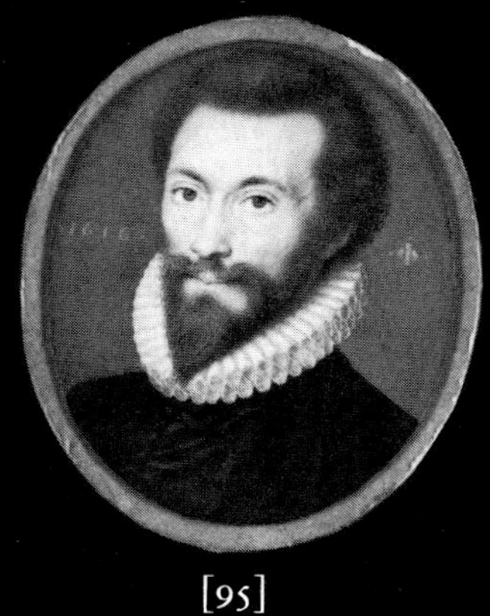

[95]

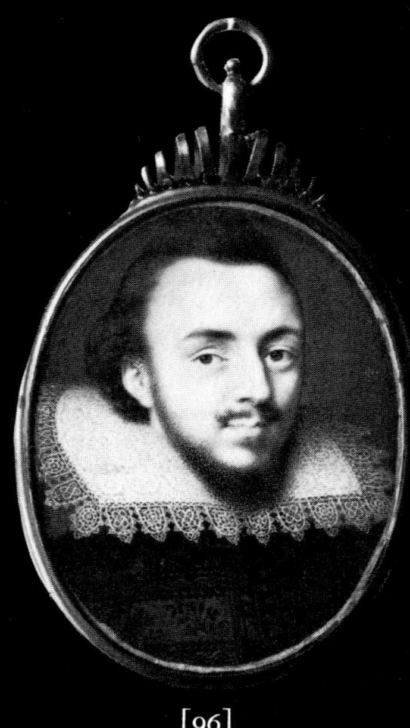

[96]

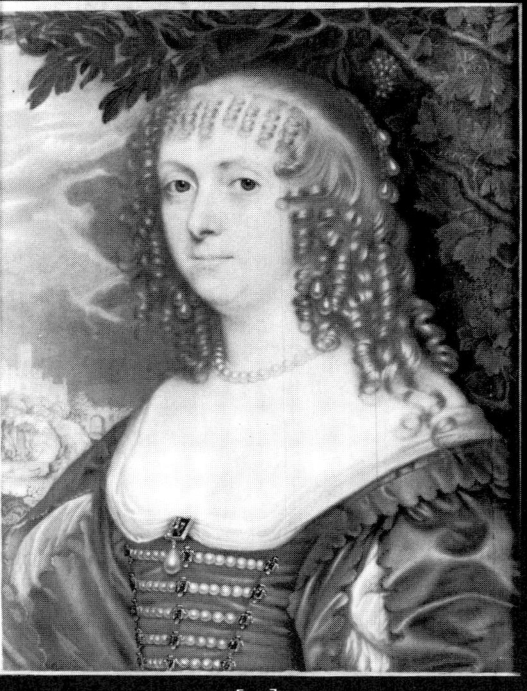

[97]

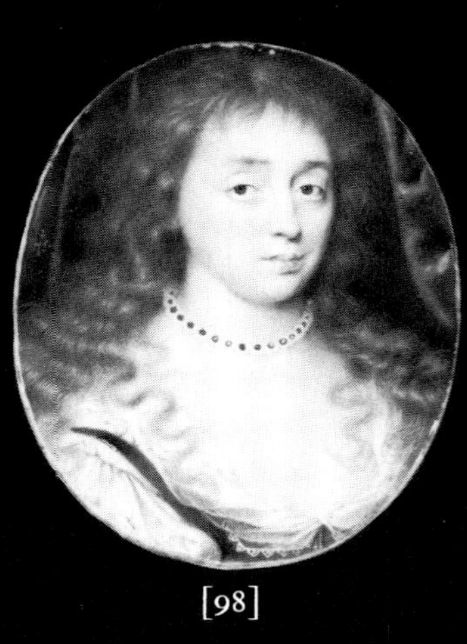

[98]

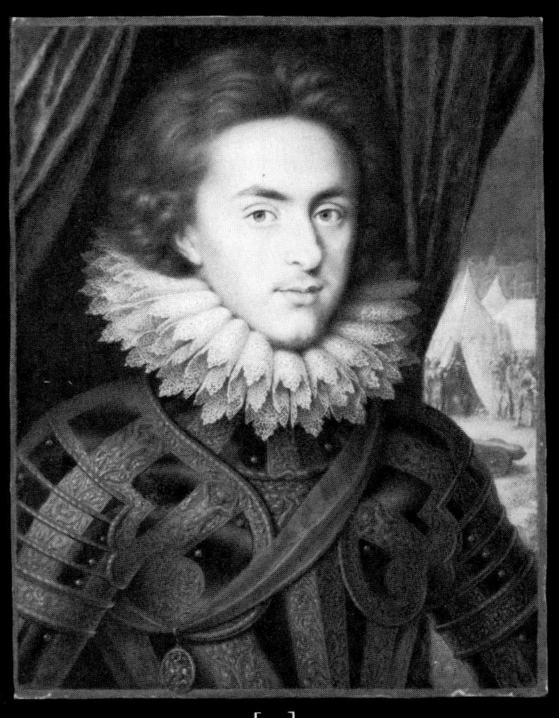

[99]

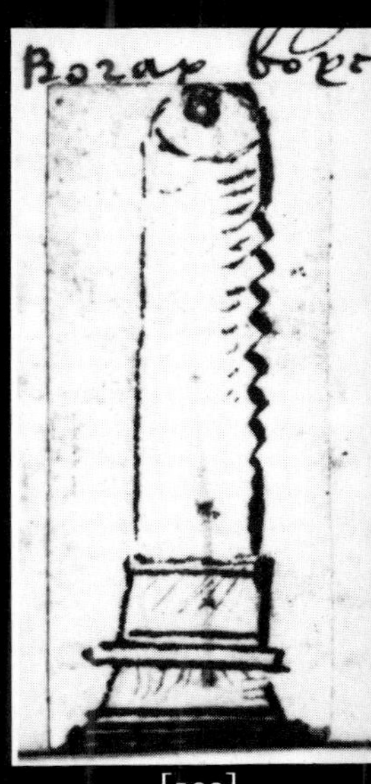

[100]

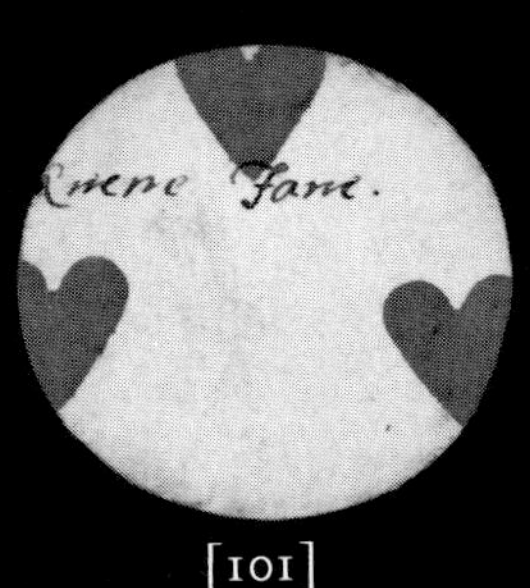

[101]

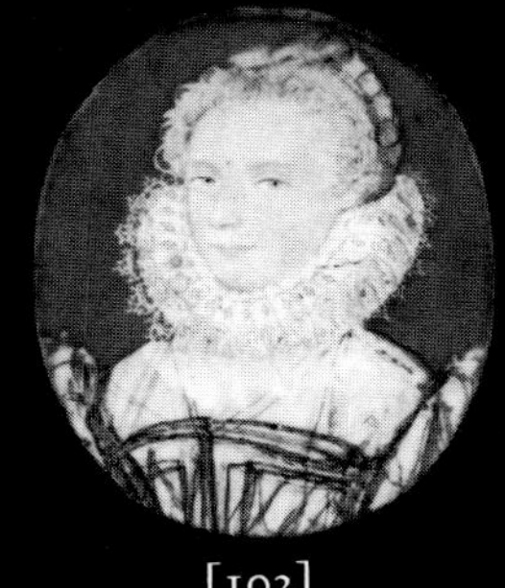

[102]

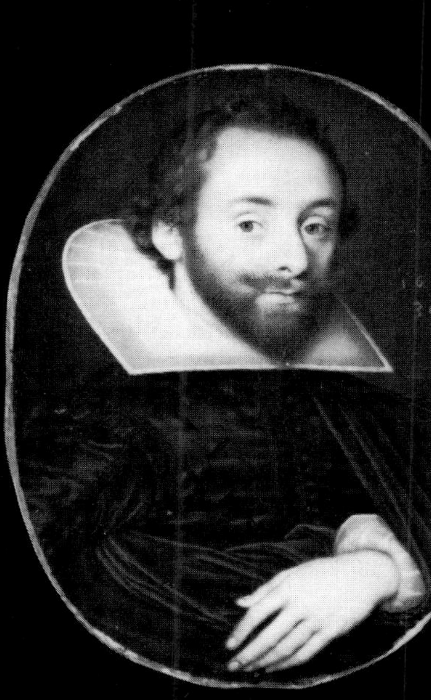

[103]

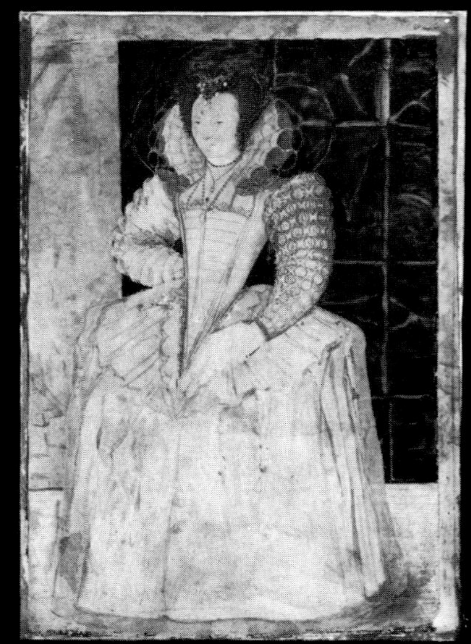

[104]

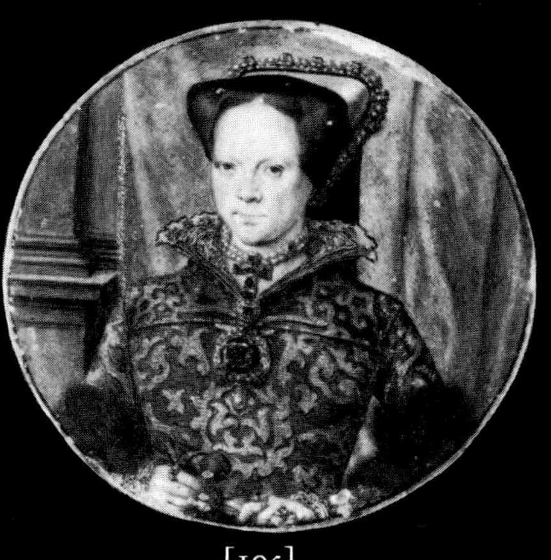

[105]

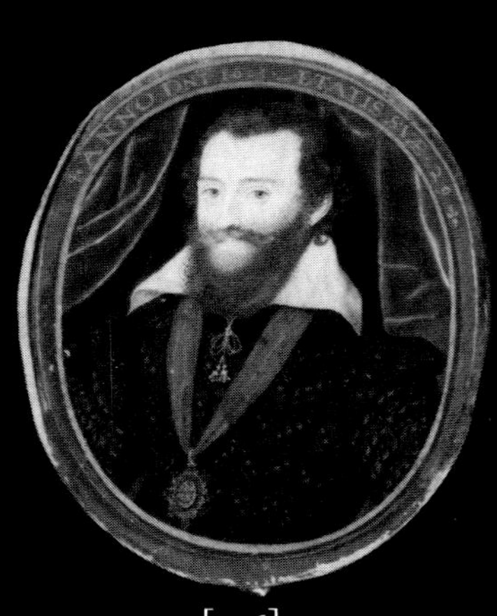

[106]

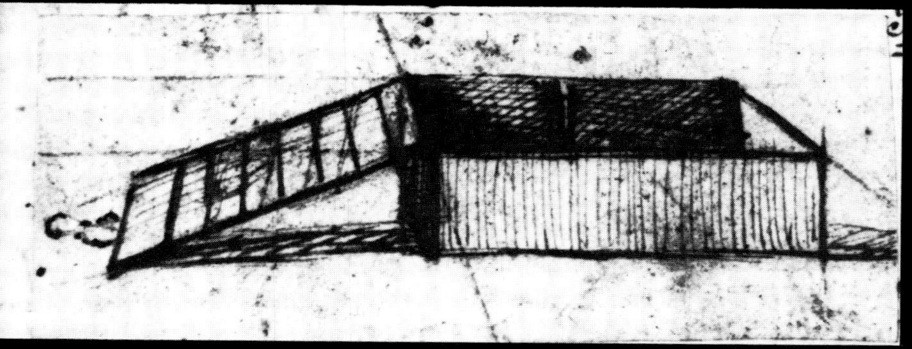

[107]

THE PLATES

(Unless otherwise indicated the miniatures are painted with watercolours on vellum stuck to card)

Frontispiece Hans Holbein the Younger. *An unknown youth,* c. 1540. Circular: 36.5mm. diameter (enlarged). By gracious permission of H.R.H. Princess Juliana of the Netherlands.

Colour plate Nicholas Hilliard. *Queen Elizabeth I,* c. 1597. Oval 65 × 51mm. Photomicrographs of (A) the face; (B) a ruby; (C) pearls; (D) lace. Victoria and Albert Museum.

1. Lucas Horenbout (c.1490/5–1544). *Henry VIII,* 1525–6. Rectangular: 53 × 48 mm, The Fitzwilliam Museum.
2. Lucas Horenbout. *Henry VIII, bearded,* 1525–6. Circular: 48 mm diameter, The Royal Collection.
3. Lucas Horenbout. *Henry VIII, beardless,* 1525–6. Circular: 40 mm diameter, The Royal Collection.
4. Lucas Horenbout. *Henry VIII,* 1525–6. Circular: 48 mm diameter, The Duke of Buccleuch.
5. Lucas Horenbout. *Katharine of Aragon,* c.1525–6. Circular: 38 mm diameter, The Duke of Buccleuch.
6. Lucas Horenbout. *Katharine of Aragon with a marmoset,* c.1525–6. Rectangular: 54.5 × 48 mm, The Duke of Buccleuch.
7. Lucas Horenbout. *Henry VIII,* c.1530. Circular: 30 mm diameter. Collection V de S.
8. Lucas Horenbout. *Lady Margaret Beaufort.* Circular: 30 mm diameter. Collection V de S.
9. Lucas Horenbout. *Possibly Anne Boleyn,* c.1532–33. Circular: 41 mm diameter. The Duke of Buccleuch.
10. Lucas Horenbout. *Edward VI,* c.1541–2. Originally circular: 34 mm diameter. The Duke of Buccleuch.
11. Lucas Horenbout. *Henry Fitzroy, Duke of Richmond,* c.1534–5. Circular: 43 mm diameter. The Royal Collection.
12. Lucas Horenbout. *Henry VIII,* c.1537. Circular: 49 mm diameter. Private Collection.
13. Lucas Horenbout. *Hans Holbein the Younger,* after a self-portrait. Circular: 42 mm diameter. The Wallace Collection.

14. Hans Holbein the Younger. *Charles Brandon*, 1541. Circular: 57 mm diameter. The Royal Collection.
15. Hans Holbein the Younger. *Henry Brandon*, 1535. Circular: 57 mm diameter. The Royal Collection.
16. Hans Holbein the Younger. *Anne of Cleves*, c.1539. Circular: 46 mm diameter. Victoria and Albert Museum.
17. Hans Holbein the Younger. *Mrs Pemberton*, c.1536. Circular: 52 mm diameter. Victoria and Albert Museum.
18. Hans Holbein the Younger. *Lord Abergavenny*, c.1535. Circular: 49 mm diameter. The Duke of Buccleuch.
19. Hans Holbein the Younger. *Unknown youth*. Circular: 36.5 mm diameter. The Royal Collection of the Netherlands.
20. Hans Holbein the Younger. *Lady Audley*, c.1540. Circular: 57 mm diameter. The Royal Collection.
21. Hans Holbein the Younger. *A lady*, called *Catherine Howard*, c.1540. Circular: 64 mm diameter. The Royal Collection.
22. Lucas Horenbout. *Henry VIII*, 1525–6. Detail. Circular: 40 mm diameter. The Royal Collection.
23. Hans Holbein the Younger. *Charles Brandon*, 1541. Detail. Circular: 57 mm diameter. The Royal Collection.
24. Nicholas Hilliard. Detail of *Richard Hilliard*, dated 1577. Circular: 41 mm diameter. Victoria and Albert Museum.
25. Albrecht Dürer. A mechanical device for drawing portraits; an illustration from his 'underweysung der messung', 1525. Woodcut.
26. Hans Holbein the Younger. *Mary, Duchess of Richmond*, 1534–6. Drawing on pink prepared paper, with black and coloured chalks, and some black wash. Rectangular: 266 × 199 mm. The Royal Collection.
27. Hans Holbein the Younger. *Sir Henry Guildford*, c.1526. Drawing on paper with black and coloured chalks, with some watercolour. Rectangular: 384 × 295 mm. The Royal Collection.
28. Hans Holbein the Younger. *Sir Richard Southwell*, 1536. Drawing on pink prepared paper with black and coloured chalks, ink, and silver point. Rectangular: 366 × 277 mm. The Royal Collection.
29. Anonymous Flemish artist. Detail of angels from a Book of Hours. Watercolour on vellum. British Library (MS. Add. 35314).
30. Anonymous Flemish artist. Detail of a head of Christ. Watercolour of vellum. British Library (MS. Add. 35313).

31. Anonymous Flemish artist. The Infanta Juaña of Spain with St. John, from a Book of Hours. Watercolour on vellum. British Library (MS. Add. 18852).
32. Anonymous Flemish artist. Detail of a pendant locket containing a miniature of Christ from a Book of Hours. Watercolour on vellum. British Library (MS. Add. 35313).
33. Levina Teerlinc. *Lady Katharine Grey*, c.1555–60. Circular: 33 mm diameter. Victoria and Albert Museum.
34. Levina Teerlinc. *Unknown lady, possibly Elizabeth I as a Princess*, c.1550. Circular: 48 mm diameter. Yale Center for British Art.
35. Levina Teerlinc. *Unknown man*, 1569. Oval: 39 × 32 mm. The Countess Beauchamp.
36. Levina Teerlinc. *Unknown man in an armillary sphere*, 1569. Circular: 39 mm diameter. The National Trust, Waddesdon Manor.
37. Simon Benninck. *Self-portrait*, 1558. Rectangular: 81 × 53 mm. Victoria and Albert Museum.
38. Levina Teerlinc. *An Elizabethan Maundy*, c.1565. Oval, cut from a rectangle: 70 × 64 mm. The Countess Beauchamp.
39. Levina Teerlinc. *Mary I Laying on hands for the King's Evil*, from Mary Tudor's Manual. Watercolour on vellum. Westminster Cathedral.
40. Levina Teerlinc. *Queen Elizabeth I*, a detail from an Indenture between Elizabeth I and the Dean and Canons of St. George's Chapel, Windsor, 1559. Watercolour on vellum. The Public Record Office, London (E.36/77).
41. Nicholas Hilliard. *Queen Elizabeth I in Robes of State*, c.1600. Rectangular: 91 × 56 mm. Private Collection.
42. Nicholas Hilliard. *Queen Elizabeth I*, a detail from the Mildmay Charter, 1584. Watercolour on vellum. Emmanuel College, Cambridge.
43. Supposedly by Nicholas Hilliard. *Self-portrait at the age of 13*, 1560. Circular: 24 mm diameter. Private Collection.
44. Nicholas Hilliard. *Self-portrait*, 1577. Circular: 41 mm diameter. Victoria and Albert Museum.
45. Nicholas Hilliard. *Edward Seymour, Duke of Somerset*, dated 1560. Circular: 33.5 mm diameter. The Duke of Buccleuch.
46. Nicholas Hilliard. *A gentleman, called Oliver St. John, 1st Baron Bletsho*, 1571. Circular: 45 mm diameter. Private Collection.

47. Nicholas Hilliard. *An unknown man, 24 in 1572.* Rectangular: 60 × 47 mm. Victoria and Albert Museum.
48. Nicholas Hilliard. *An unknown lady, 52 in 1572.* Circular: 49 mm diameter. The Duke of Buccleuch.
49. Nicholas Hilliard. *Jane Boughton,* 1574. Circular: 44 mm diameter. Private Collection.
50. Nicholas Hilliard. *An unknown man, 37 in 1574.* Circular: 40 mm diameter. The Fitzwilliam Museum.
51. Nicholas Hilliard. *An unknown lady,* 1575. Circular: 45 mm diameter. The Mauritshuis, Hague.
52. Nicholas Hilliard. *Queen Elizabeth I,* c.1575. Oval: 18 × 15 mm. Mrs E. Hamilton.
53. Nicholas Hilliard. *Robert Dudley, Earl of Essex,* c.1575. Oval: 18.5 × 15 mm. Mrs E. Hamilton.
54. Nicholas Hilliard. *Duc d'Alençon,* c.1567. Oval: 45 × 37 mm. Kunsthistorisches Museum, Vienna.
55. Nicholas Hilliard. *Alice Hilliard,* 1578. Circular: 59 mm diameter. Victoria and Albert Museum.
56. Nicholas Hilliard. *Sir Henry Slingsby,* 1595. Oval: 84 × 63 mm. The Fitzwilliam Museum.
57. Nicholas Hilliard. *James I,* c.1604. Oval: 53 × 43 mm. Victoria and Albert Museum.
58. Nicholas Hilliard. *Charles I as a youth,* c.1611. Oval: 51 × 41 mm. Victoria and Albert Museum.
59. Nicholas Hilliard. *Henry VIII,* after Holbein, c.1600. Circular: 31 mm diameter. The Royal Collection.
60. Nicholas Hilliard. *Edward Seymour, Duke of Somerset,* c.1600. Circular: 34 mm diameter. Victoria and Albert Museum.
61. Nicholas Hilliard. *A lady, called Queen Elizabeth I,* c.1600. Circular: 40 mm diameter. Private Collection.
62. Nicholas Hilliard. *Queen Elizabeth I,* c.1585. Drawing on paper with graphite and pen. Rectangular: 137 × 160 mm. Victoria and Albert Museum.
63. Isaac Oliver (died 1617). *Queen Elizabeth I,* c.1595, a pattern miniature. Oval: 62 × 53 mm. Victoria and Albert Museum.
64. Isaac Oliver. *Queen Elizabeth I,* c.1595. Oval: 49 × 39 mm. Formerly in the Heckett Collection.

65. Isaac Oliver. *Charles I as a youth*, a pattern miniature after 1611. Oval: 51 × 40 mm. Private Collection.
66. Isaac Oliver. *Robert Devereux, Earl of Essex*, c.1595, a pattern miniature. Oval: 53 × 43 mm. Yale Center for British Art. Paul Mellon Collection.
67. Rowland Lockey (c.1565/7–1616). *The Family of Sir Thomas More*, c.1600, detail of the right-hand group. Rectangular: 241 × 292 mm. Victoria and Albert Museum.
68. Rowland Lockey. *Sir Francis Walsingham*, c.1580. Oval: 43 × 73 mm. The Duke of Buccleuch.
69. Lawrence Hilliard (1581/2–1647/8). *An unknown woman*, c.1610. Oval: 55 × 46 mm. Victoria and Albert Museum.
70. Isaac Oliver. *An unknown woman 20 in 1587*. Oval: 55 × 44 mm. The Duke of Buccleuch.
71. Isaac Oliver. *Self-portrait*, c.1588. Oval: 45 × 36 mm. The Royal Collection.
72. Isaac Oliver. *An unknown man 57 in 1588*. Oval: 54 × 49 mm. The Fitzwilliam Museum.
73. Isaac Oliver. *A young man aged 19 in 1588*. Oval: 51 × 42 mm. Brinsley Ford, Esq.
74. Isaac Oliver. *A small girl holding an apple, aged 5 in 1590*. Oval: 54 × 41 mm. Victoria and Albert Museum.
75. Nicholas Hilliard. *George Clifford, Earl of Cumberland*. Rectangular: 258 × 176 mm. The National Maritime Museum.
76. Nicholas Hilliard. *Robert Devereux, Earl of Essex*, c.1595(?) Rectangular: 251 × 203 mm. Private Collection.
77. Isaac Oliver. *A melancholy young man*, c.1590–5. Rectangular: 125 × 88 mm. The Royal Collection.
78. Isaac Oliver. *A lady formerly called Lucy Harington*, c.1605. Circular: 127 mm diameter. The Fitzwilliam Museum.
79. Isaac Oliver. *Richard Sackville, Earl of Dorset*, 1616. Rectangular: 235 × 153 mm. Victoria and Albert Museum.
80. Isaac Oliver. *Allegory of Love*, c.1610? Rectangular: 111 × 171 mm. The Royal Museum of Fine Arts, Copenhagen.
81. Nicholas Hilliard. *Henry Percy, Earl of Northumberland*, c.1595. Rectangular: 257 × 172 mm. Rijksmuseum, Amsterdam.

82. Isaac Oliver. Compositional sketch for *A lady formerly called Lucy Harington*, c.1605? Pen and ink on paper. Rectangular: 149 × 111 mm. The Fitzwilliam Museum.
83. Isaac Oliver. *Nymphs and satyrs*, c.1610–15? Black and white chalk on brown paper. Rectangular: 205 × 357 mm. The Royal Collection.
84. Isaac Oliver. *Unknown Melancholy Young Man, called 'The Prodigal Son'*, c.1595. Oval: 72 × 52 mm. Private Collection.
85. Nicholas Hilliard. *Young man amongst roses, probably Robert Devereux, Earl of Essex*, c.1587. Oval: 136 × 73 mm. Victoria and Albert Museum.
86. Isaac Oliver. *Moses striking the rock*. Drawing on paper in mixed media. Rectangular: 210 × 333 mm. The Royal Collection.
87. Isaac Oliver. *The Adoration of the Magi*. Mixed media on paper. Rectangular: 229 × 168 mm. The British Museum, Department of Prints and Drawings.
88. Isaac Oliver. *Lord Herbert of Cherbury*, c.1610–14. Rectangular: 230 × 189 mm. The Earl of Powis.
89. Isaac Oliver. *Diederik Sonoy*, 1588. Rectangular: 68 × 55 mm. The Royal Collection of the Netherlands.
90. Isaac Oliver. *Unknown lady*, c.1590. Oval: 60 × 50 mm. The Fitzwilliam Museum.
91. Isaac Oliver. Detail of *A lady, said to be Frances Howard, Countess of Essex and Somerset*, c.1596–1600. Circular: 130 mm diameter. The Victoria and Albert Museum.
92. Isaac Oliver. *The Brothers Browne*, 1598. Rectangular: 240 × 260 mm. Burghley House.
93. Isaac Oliver. *Head of Christ*, c.1615–17. Oval: 53 × 43 mm. Victoria and Albert Museum.
94. Isaac Oliver. *Sir Richard Leveson*. Oval: 54 × 45 mm. Private Collection.
95. Isaac Oliver. *Dr John Donne*, 1616. Oval: 44 × 36 mm. The Royal Collection.
96. Isaac Oliver. *An unknown man*, 1610. Oval: 54 × 41 mm. Victoria and Albert Museum.
97. John Hoskins (c.1590–1664–5). *Catherine Bruce, Countess of Dysart*, 1638. Rectangular: 229 × 174 mm. Ham House.

98. John Hoskins. *An unknown lady, called Lady Shirley*, c.1630. Oval: 54 × 44 mm. Private Collection.
99. Isaac Oliver. *Henry Frederick, Prince of Wales*, c.1612. Rectangular: 130 × 102 mm. The Royal Collection.
100. Anon. A drawing of a dispenser for powders from the manuscript by a pupil of Nicholas Hilliard. Pen and ink on paper. MS. Harl. 6376. British Library, Department of Manuscripts.
101. Verso of a miniature showing the playing card.
102. Nicholas Hilliard. *A lady*, unfinished, c.1575–80. Oval: 39 × 33 mm. Victoria and Albert Museum.
103. Isaac Oliver. *Unknown man*, 1614. Oval: 57 × 41 mm. The Royal Collection of the Netherlands.
104. Nicholas Hilliard. *Unknown lady*, unfinished. Rectangular: 185 × 126 mm. The Fitzwilliam Museum.
105. Hans Eworth (fl.1540–75). *Queen Mary I*, c.1555. Oil on gold. Circular: 56 mm diameter. The Duke of Buccleuch.
106. Studio of Nicholas Hilliard. *Ludovick Stuart, Duke of Lennox and Richmond*, c.1610. Oval: 52 × 43 mm. Private Collection.
107. Anon. A drawing of a portable paint box and easel from the manuscript by a pupil of Nicholas Hilliard. Pen and ink on paper. MS. Harl. 6376. British Library, Department of Manuscripts.

PART II

The Limner in his Studio

In describing the studio practices of the average *miniature painter in the sixteenth and early seventeenth centuries I shall, as far as possible, indicate where individual artists may have diverged from the norm as discussed in manuscript sources. The earliest is Hilliard's treatise, while the latest is the second version of Norgate's work written in c.1648, which harks back to the glories of Oliver and Hilliard. The quotations from Hilliard's treatise have been drawn from the invaluable new publication of the Edinburgh University manuscript (Laing 111, 174) edited by R. K. R. Thornton and T. G. S. Cain,* The Arte of Limning, *1981. The source for Norgate's first treatise is the British Library MS. Harley 6000, which is entitled* An exact & Compendious Discours concerning the Art of Miniatura or Limning, the names. Nature & proparties of the Collours, the orders to be observed in preparing & using them both for Picture by the Life, Landscape & Historyes. *I have had the good fortune to be able to use the transcript of this manuscript made by my friend, Jeffrey Muller, with whom I am editing a forthcoming work on the Norgate treatises. For Norgate's second treatise, contained in the Bodleian Library MS. Tann. 326, the transcript edited and published by Martin Hardie,* MINIATURA or The Art of Limning by EDWARD NORGATE, *1919, is of unchallengeable excellence. The last manuscript which has been used as a source for this chapter is the British Library MS. Harley 6376, which for too long has remained unrecognised as a valuable compendium of sixteenth and early seventeenth century studio methods.*

This manuscript has been attributed to Henry Gyles (1645–1709) on the basis of inscriptions at the beginning and end of the work and has therefore been known as the 'Gyles manuscript'. The latter part of the manuscript was written by Gyles himself but the earlier sections dealing with miniature and oil painting are written in a different hand. The inscription on the fly-leaf ('Henry Gyles Booke') is not a claim to authorship but to ownership. The early part of the manuscript cannot possibly have been composed by Gyles because it contains a number of references to Nicholas Hilliard's tutelage which are not contained in any other manuscript, and therefore must have been written by an artist who was receiving instruction from Hilliard at least twenty-six years before Gyles was born. Although the format and much of the wording are largely taken from Norgate's first treatise there is a great deal of additional material, some of which derives from the experience and observations of a practising miniaturist; while there is much information on Hilliard's studio methods which is not included by Norgate in either of his treaties, nor by Hilliard in his manuscript. Moreover, the author was able to quote Hilliard verbatim, *giving him the rare distinction of having had access to Hilliard's manuscript as well as Norgate's. The accounts of Hilliard's methods argue a close studio relationship and usually include phrases such as 'as he taught me', 'this secret I had of Master Hillyard', and 'Old Mr Hillyard's way was always. . .'. The author was instructed in miniature painting by Hilliard but was taught oil painting by another artist whom he describes as 'my Master Mr Martins the elder'. This is probably an anglicisation of Daniel Mytens the Elder. An interesting link emerges, for Mytens' first patron in this country was the second Earl of Arundel, who also employed Norgate as writing master to his sons (Norgate's second treatise was dedicated to his former charge, the third Earl). Norgate knew Hilliard and his studio and must also have known Mytens. Quite possibly Norgate recommended to Mytens a talented young man he had met in Hilliard's studio, a young man who was so highly regarded that he had access to both Hilliard's and Norgate's manuscripts.*

The author describes Hilliard's later method of painting red curtain backgrounds, so he must have been in Hilliard's studio after 1600. He implied that he preferred the earlier 'wet-in-wet' technique and said that his own method was to add blue to the lake to make a deeper purplish red. The manuscript reveals that the author was a prolific professional miniaturist, unlike Norgate, who had practised limning for his 'recreation as [his] better employment gave [him] leave'. The sequence of the manuscript and the greater emphasis on the art of limming suggest that he was trained as an easel painter but had concentrated his energies on miniature painting. In spite of his evident respect for Hilliard he was sufficiently confident to recommend his own methods as an alternative to the older man's.

Sources of information

The author was a professional miniaturist who had been trained by Hilliard but who had also been taught easel painting by another artist, probably Mytens. He wrote the manuscript after 1620, the date of Norgate's first treatise upon which it is based, and was presumably practising from about then onwards. We also know that he painted curtain backgrounds in a peculiarly deep bluish crimson using Hilliard's earlier type of handling. There is only one artist who fits the description – John Hoskins.

We know little about Hoskins' early life but he was born c.1590 and could have been trained by Hilliard and, subsequently, Mytens. If the Martins/Mytens hypothesis is correct it is interesting that Hoskins' images of Charles I in c.1627 were based on a Mytens original[1]*. From* The Art of Painting, *1706, a translation of de Pile's work with additional biographies of English artists we learn that Hoskins was 'bred a Face-Painter in Oil, but afterwards taking to* Miniature, *he far exceeded what he did before'. There is no evidence that he was taught by Hilliard apart from his miniatures of the 1620s in which, as John Murdoch has noticed 'the confidence and neatness of Hoskins's performance [of Hilliard's unique painting techniques] tend to suggest that he may have learned at first hand in Hilliard's studio*[2]*. He was also known to Norgate who described him in his second treatise as one of the 'doctors' of limning. Furthermore Hoskins's red curtain backgrounds in his earlier miniatures* are *painted with a peculiarly dark purplish red in Hilliard's earlier 'wet-in-wet' technique. There is a final clue on the last page of the miniature and oil sections of the manuscript, before it is continued in Gyles's hand. This is the date 1664, written in a hand other than Gyles's. It is the date of John Hoskins's death.*

In the following chapter and its notes the four treatises will be described as 'Hilliard', 'Norgate I', 'Norgate II' (in chronological sequence), and the 'Hilliard Studio MS'.

---

1. See Murdoch in Murdoch, Murrell, Noon and Strong, *The English Miniature*, 1981, p. 98.
2. Ibid., p. 97.

ALTHOUGH THE LIMNER could paint in a limited space, it was necessary that his workroom should be large to place the sitter at six yards distance for a full-length portrait, and it was important to observe certain rules regarding climate and light. It was essential that the limner should be fastidious about cleanliness, especially in choosing his room, which should be 'a warme Chamber free from dust and smoake and the Sulphrous aire of Sea cole'[3]. It was Hilliard who first observed the effect of sulphurous pollution on pigments: '. . . the culers them sellves may not endure some ayers, especially in the sulphirous ayre of seacole, and the guilding of Gowldsmithes. .'[4]. Sea coal was so named because it was mined in the north and shipped from Newcastle to London. It was a convenient replacement for timber which was becoming scarcer because of deforestation; but it was unpleasant to use in fireplaces designed for log-burning[5]. Sulphurous pollution was probably as high inside the house as it was outside. Light was also important. North light is traditionally the best for painting because of the absence of direct sunlight and the resulting diffused and uniform quality. In Hilliard's words '. . . let your light be northward, somewhat toward the east which commly is without sune, *shininge* in, on[e] only light great and faire let it be, and without impeachment, or reflections, of walls, or trees, a free sky light the dieper the window and farer, the better, and no by window, but a cleare story. .'[6]. Later he commented on the difference between easel painting and limning; that a picture which was to be viewed from a distance required the stronger shadows produced by a small high light, whereas a miniature should have little shadow. He quoted Lomazzo who said that shadow was '. . . but the defect of light. . .'[7]. This preference for a diffused light

3. Hilliard Studio MS., p. 8.
4. Hilliard, p. 74.
5. For the horrors of pollution in seventeenth century London, see John Evelyn. *Fumifugium: or The Inconveniencie of the Aer and Smoak of London Dissipated.* 1661.
6. Hilliard, pp. 72–74.

in which the features could be modelled with very little deepening of the shadows was not new in limning, for the miniatures of Horenbout, Holbein and Teerlinc are all worked in this manner, and it was certainly no novelty to Hilliard who had always imitated Holbein's manner of limning[8]; so his reference to Queen Elizabeth wanting an '. . . open ally of a goodly garden. . .' in which to pose – a choice, he asserted, showing superior judgement – was the purest sycophancy[9]. As well as a fawner he was a name-dropper and a social climber, a braggadocio with pretensions to rise above the artisan level, and his failures are frequently recorded with extreme bitterness. On the other hand he was unable to sacrifice excellence for profit, was generous to his friends and was adventurous and improvident.

It is on shadowing in limning that Hilliard and Oliver part company, for until the end of his life the former modelled the features of his sitters with scant use of tone while Oliver, once he had become independent of his instructor, frequently modelled his faces with strong *chiaroscuro*, especially in his works of the 'eighties and 'nineties. One can presume that Oliver either limited the light in his studio to a small high source or used his considerable talent for artistic invention to exaggerate the very slight shadows which can be seen in diffused illumination.

The limner, because of the scale and vulnerability of his work, was faced with extraordinary demands on his self-discipline. He was required to wear silken clothes which would not shed dust or hairs on his work and was enjoined by Hilliard to 'tuch not your worke with your fingers, or any hard thing, but with a cleane pencel brush it, or with a whit feather, neither breathe one it, especially in could weather, take heed of the dandrawe of the head sheading from the haire, and of speaking over your worke for sparkling, for the least sparling of spettel, will never be holpen if it light in the face. . .'[10].

7. Ibid., p. 88.
8. Ibid., p. 68.
9. Ibid., pp. 84–86.
10. Ibid., p. 72.

Self-discipline did not end with the sittings for Hilliard exhorted the artist to be temperate in all things so he might be in fit condition to pursue this talent for '. . . thosse surly which have such a guift of god ought to rejoyce with humble thankfulnes and to be very wary and temperat in diet and other goverment, least it be sone taken from them againe by some sudaine mischance, or by their evell coustomes, their sight, or stedines of hand decay. . .'[11]. He warned '. . sleepe not much, wacth not much, eat not much, sit not long, usse not violent excersize in sports, nor ea[r]nest for your recreation but dancing or bowling, or littel of either. . .'[12]. A crumb of comfort was extended to the limner in a later printed book where it was suggested that 'Flowers of *Burrage*, and leaves of *Burnet*, put into *French-wine*, the colours comfort the *eyes*, the property of the *Herbs* represse the vapour of the *Wine*; and this *Wine* is most due to be drunk by an excellent *Painter*; in which, other persons may have leave to taste onely, unlesse to drink his health. . .'[13].

After the condition for the studio most treatises discuss the pigments which were to be used, and the way in which they were to be prepared. Limners were fastidious and assiduous in the selection and preparation of their pigments, which were mainly obtained from the apothecary[14] although a very few colours were still manufactured in the artist's studio in order to ensure their excellence and freedom from the adulterations common to the sharp practice of the period[15]. But they did reject some pigments commonly used in other types of painting. Hilliard and Norgate recommended surprisingly large palettes. The works of Horenbout, Holbein and Teerlinc show that they were even more selective in their choice of pigments and their palettes were extremely restricted. To assemble a putative list of the

---

11. Ibid., p. 64.
12. Ibid., p. 72.
13. William Sanderson. *Graphice*, 1658, p. 87.
14. Anon. *A Very Proper Treatise, wherein is briefly set forth the arte of limming. . .*, 1573, f.xii.
15. D. V. Thompson. *The Materials of Medieval Painting*, 1936, *passim*.

colours Horenbout used one must rely on visual appearance and the use of x-radiography, infra-red and ultra-violet reflectance, coupled with intelligent deduction[16]. X-radiography shows that there were two white pigments; one was white lead and the other probably the same chalk-like ceruse which Hilliard later used. Surface examination and infra-red reflectance demonstrate that there were two black pigments, both of which were types of carbon. From their appearance and the evidence of contemporary usage it seems probably that one was lamp black and the other ivory black[17]. The red which can be seen to advantage in the spandrels of the Fitzwilliam *Henry VIII* (Pl. 1) was certainly vermilion, and this colour, rather than red lead, was used in modelling the features. Horenbout's yellows were predominantly types of ochre, although massicot[18] may have been employed on occasion. The brilliant blue used for the backgrounds is revealed by infra-red reflectance to be a copper carbonate and is almost certainly the natural pigment known as blue bice, prepared from the mineral azurite. In some of the miniatures there is copper green, most probably green bice, which was prepared from another mineral form of copper carbonate, malachite. There may well have been a few more pigments on Horenbout's palette. However, it is clear from studies of his works that Horenbout used far fewer colours than those listed by Hilliard in his treatise. Before itemising those colours which were to be used for limning[19], Hilliard mentioned others which were to be eschewed. Orpiment, verdigris, verditer, pink, sap-green and litmus were rejected on the grounds that they were either 'ill-smelling' or 'illtasting', or 'unsweet'. Hilliard's rather subjective condemnation on the basis of taste or smell is supported

16. For more detailed information on pigments see R. J. Gettens and G. L. Stout, *Painting Materials*, 1942, and Dr R. D. Harley *Artists' Pigments c.1600–1835*, 1970.
17. Limming, 1573, *op. cit.*, ff.vi b and vii.
18. Recent research suggests that the pigment massicot was a lead-tin yellow rather than a lead oxide. For further detail on this point see R. D. Harley, *op. cit.*, pp. 85–86.
19. Hilliard, pp. 90–95.

by more modern, scientific reasoning. The brilliant yellow orpiment is a very poisonous colour made from arsenic and sulphur and, quite apart from its obvious danger to the artist – frequently drawing the brush between his lips to maintain its point – it mixes badly with a number of other pigments, causing discolouration. Verdigris, the green which results from the corrosion of copper has a tendency to discolour from green to brown, is a poor mixer, and has been known to eat its way through the parchment of manuscripts[20]. Pink was a yellow to brown pigment made from the dyestuffs of certain plants. In Hilliard's day its manufacture was uncertain although later varieties, such as that made by Sir Nathaniel Bacon[21], were considered to be dependable. But all pinks had a tendency to fade in watercolour. Litmus blue was not only very fugitive but also had the disadvantage that it changed to red in the presence of acid. Later in his treatise, however, Hilliard recommended verditer[22], sap-green[23], pink and litmus[24] for certain purposes. Although he regarded them as deplorable they were evidently a necessary evil.

To simplify the complex subject of Hilliard's extensive palette, I have extracted the following list of pigments from the treatise.

WHITES

Ceruse	White Lead

The term ceruse has been the cause of a great deal of confusion as it has been used at various periods to indicate quite different pigments. In the seventeenth century it was frequently used to describe

---

20. D. V. Thompson, *op. cit.*, p. 165.
21. Sir Nathaniel Bacon's pink is praised and recipes are supplied in various seventeenth century treatises.
22. Verditer was a manufactured copper pigment which could vary in hue from bright blue to green, depending on the mode of manufacture. It was not a dependable pigment.
23. Sap green was made from various dyes from plants and was a very fugitive colour.
24. Litmus is a dye rather than a pigment. Extracted from lichen and used as a transparent blue watercolour it has the inherent disadvantage of changing to red in the presence of acid.

a white pigment which contained lead white, while in the eighteenth century lead white and ceruse became synonymous. Hilliard made it quite clear that he was discussing two different pigments and that ceruse could be made in three grades, the coarsest of which was to be used for the carnation. This tallies with the evidence of X-radiographs of Hilliard's miniatures where the ruffs and ancillary parts of the miniature can be seen to be painted with white lead, while the carnation is certainly painted with a colour of low atomic weight, possibly composed mainly of chalk[25].

YELLOWS
Massicot[26]
Yellow ochre[27]
Ochre de Russe[28]
Gallstone[29]
Pink[30]
Yellow from rose petals[31]
Saffron[32]

MURREYS
Venice Lake[33]
Antwerp Lake

REDS
Indian Lake[34]
Red lead[35]
Vermilion[36]

BLUES
Bice[37]
Smalt[38]
Ultramarine[39]
Indigo[40]
Litmus[41]
Florey[42]

GREENS
Ceder green[43]
Verditer[44]
Sap-green[45]
Pansy green[46]

BROWNS
Cologne earth[47]
Umber[48]
Asphaltum[49]

BLACKS
Soot[50]
Sea coal[51]
Velvet black[52]
Cherry stone black[53]
Date stone black
Peach black
Charcoal black[54]

METALS
Silver
Gold

25. X-rays are absorbed by compounds of high molecular weight, such as lead white, producing white areas on the X-radiographic film; whereas pigments which are easily penetrated, like calcium carbonate (chalk), appear as dark patches.

26. Massicot was a pigment which could be obtained in a variety of bright yellow hues. See note 17 above.
27. Yellow ochre, an iron oxide, can vary considerably in colour depending on its natural source.
28. Probably a dark yellow iron oxide. See R. D. Harley, *op. cit.*, pp. 82–83.
29. When prepared from crushed ox gall-stones this was probably a deep, transparent yellow colour. It should *not* be confused with the substitute made from ox bile.
30. The modern connotation of the word 'pink' is that of a pale red colour. In the sixteenth and seventeenth centuries it signified a yellow to dark yellow pigment made by staining chalk or alum with a plant dye. See R. D. Harley, *op. cit.*, pp. 97–101.
31. It is impossible to know what sort of colour this would have been. Presumably it was a stain rather than a pigment unless it was, like pink, used to stain a solid body such as chalk or alum. However it was prevalent and one must assume that it was an extremely fugitive colour.
32. The bright yellow made from the *crocus* was employed purely as a stain and was thus used as a transparent toning colour over another solid body of yellow pigment, rather than independently. It is very fugitive.
33. Venice and Antwerp lakes were the colours which Hilliard described as murreys and which he likened to the precious stone, the amethyst. These lakes, which are uncertain in origin, but which may have been processed from the same material, were processed at the two great centres of commerce in the sixteenth century, Venice and Antwerp. For more detailed discussion see R. D. Harley, *op. cit.*, pp. 120–124.
34. It is difficult to separate Indian lake from the murrey colours discussed in Note 32. There is no doubt that it was a scarlet, rather than a crimson, colour, but its difference in origin remains obscure.
35. Red lead is an orange-red pigment made by heating white lead or by oxidising the metal itself in an oven. For further information see R. D. Harley, *op. cit.*, pp. 112–114.
36. Vermilion is a bright scarlet, generally tending towards purple, made by heating mercury and sulphur together to form mercuric sulphide. It can vary considerably in colour. In medieval times the naturally occuring form was frequently used. For more information see R. D. Harley, *op. cit.*, pp. 114–117.
37. The brilliant blue made from azurite which was normally used for the backgrounds of miniatures until the end of the sixteenth century.
38. A dull blue pigment made from cobalt blue glass. It was not much used in miniature painting because of its coarseness.
39. Genuine ultramarine is made from the rare mineral lapis lazuli which, in the sixteenth century, made the long journey to western Europe from Afghanistan via the trade centre of Venice. Hilliard's valuation of the best ultramarine at eleven pounds, ten shillings an ounce in c.1600 explains its rarity in sixteenth century limning! and its more regular appearance in miniatures of the first quarter of the sixteenth century can be explained by the development of English trade in the eastern Mediterranean. See R. D. Harley, *op. cit.*, pp. 41–43. Hilliard advised using bice

or smalt as an alternative. Infra-red reflectance shows that most of his backgrounds were painted with bice as were those of his predecessors.

40. A dark transparent blue pigment made from a plant dye imported from the Orient. For more information see R. D. Harley, *op. cit.*, pp. 62–65.
41. A blue-violet dye made from the stain from certain lichens, mixed with an alkali to fix the blue colour.
42. In ambiguous texts the term 'florey' could be taken to mean either the flower of woad or indigo. However here indigo has already been mentioned, so there is no doubt that in this case 'florey' alludes to the blue colour produced from woad. Woad was a dark blue transparent colour easily confused with indigo, sometimes stained on to a white base to make a lighter blue. See R. D. Harley, *op. cit.*, pp. 61–62.
43. Ceder green was almost certainly the name for the pigment obtained from the mineral, chrysocolla; a naturally occuring copper silicate. One may assume from the literature that it was a brighter green than malachite, a natural copper carbonate, and was difficult to obtain. For further information see R. D. Harley, *op. cit.*, pp. 70–72.
44. Verditer was a manufactured copper carbonate, either blue or green depending on its manufacture. Both the manufacture and the subsequent behaviour of the colour were very unpredictable. Presumably Hilliard was referring to a green verditer but he may have meant a blue verditer which would have been mixed with yellows to obtain various greens. For further information see R. D. Harley, *op. cit.*, pp. 72–73.
45. Although the name 'sap green' could describe a rather acid yellow-green made from various plants, the term was usually reserved for a colour made from ripe buckthorn berries. It was a very fugitive colour. For further information see R. D. Harley, *op. cit.*, pp. 79–81.
46. The stain from pansy petals was extracted and then precipitated with alum to make a very fugitive transparent pigment.
47. Cologne or Cullen's earth was a dark brown pigment made from naturally occuring lignite or peat. It was later termed Vandyke brown because Van Dyck used it extensively in his works.
48. A brown earth which has a greenish tone in its raw state. It was normally burnt for miniature painting which improved its working properties and gave it a warmer tone.
49. A dark brown made from solidified bitumen.
50. It seems probable that as Hilliard included soot amongst the dark brown shadowing colours he meant wood soot (bistre) rather than lamp soot (the black colour normally called lamp black); but see R. D. Harley, *op. cit.*, p. 144.
51. The brownish black made by grinding ordinary coal.
52. This pigment was more frequently described as ivory black and was made by charring fragments of ivory in a sealed crucible.
53. Cherry stone, date stone and peach black were made by calcining the stones of those fruits in a sealed crucible. Their colour was not so deep as that of ivory black.
54. A black with a bluish tone usually made from vine charcoal.

Pigments

In the sixteenth and early seventeenth centuries the preparation of pigments was a studio activity, undertaken by the artist or a studio assistant under supervision. In either case the artist himself would have been intimately concerned with the selection and purchase of raw materials. There were two main methods of preparing pigments to sufficient fineness – grinding and washing. They had to be extremely finely ground for miniature painting and the process was laborious. The pulverised pigment was placed on a flat stone made from porphyry, serpentine or pebble, damped with clean water and levigated using a muller made from the same material as the stone. When the pigment was sufficiently fine for limning the paste was scraped from the stone and muller and set aside to dry. When the water had evaporated the very fine powdered pigment was stored in boxes or folded papers ready for use[55].

The grinding process was inimical to some pigments, causing them to loose their richness of colour or to become slimy and unfit for painting. Such pigments were prepared by washing. This process separated the finest particles of pigment and helped remove dirt and adulterants. The pigment was first bruised to a powder and then placed in a basin of water which was shaken until the pigment particles were suspended in the water. When the pigment had fallen to the bottom of the basin any scum floating on the surface was poured away and fresh water added. The pigment was again stirred with water and before it was half settled – when the coarsest particles had sunk to the bottom – the water with the suspended pigment was poured into a second vessel and more water was added, the contents being agitated again and allowed to settle so that any further scum could be poured away. This process was repeated until no more scum rose. The water was again stirred up and the finer particles decanted into a third container, the refining being repeated several more times until the very finest pigments had been separated, dried

55. Norgate I, pp. 2–3, Norgate II, pp. 9–10, Hilliard Studio MS., p. 25.

and put away in boxes or papers ready for use[56]. Very little of the original bulk of pigment was suitable for use and 'if a hand full of Red Leade yeild a Shell or two of good and fine Colloure it is enough[57].

The colours which had to be prepared by washing were red lead, massicot, green bice (prepared from malachite), ceder green, blue bice, and smalt[58]. There was a greater concern over the preparation of the whites, particularly white lead, which had to be both ground *and* washed[59]. The best whites were selected and put in the sun before they were finely ground in the usual way. While they were wet from the grinding stone they were laid on a flat piece of chalk which would 'suck up and draw away the filth and greasiness, and many times the salt which is the greatest kind of evill and cause of spoyling the Colour'. The white lead was ground again with a solution of gum water and then washed to separate the pigment into grades and clean the colour[60]. Hilliard, with his love of variations in surface texture, used to separate his white into three grades; the coarsest for the carnation, the next for painting linen and the finest for satin[61].

Perhaps the most complicated pigment to prepare was ultramarine which became available in England at the end of the sixteenth century. The raw material, lapis lazuli, contained a number of impurities which could spoil the colour of the pigment. To produce the purest colour and separate the weaker tints, a special method of preparation was adopted. The raw mineral, broken into small pieces but still containing a large proportion of impurities, was heated in a covered pot on a charcoal fire. After an hour the particles were cast into a vessel of urine, wine vinegar or water; the resulting contrac-

56. Norgate I, p. 6–7, Norgate II, pp. 16–17, Hilliard Studio MS., pp. 32–35.
57. Norgate I, p. 6. The shell was a mussel shell.
58. Hilliard Studio MS., p. 24.
59. Ibid., p. 25.
60. Ibid., pp. 25–26.
61. Norgate II, p. 90.

tion caused further fragmentation of the mineral. The material was then dried on a shovel over the fire. The greyer parts of the material were cut away, using pincers. The lapis was then ground with a solution of honey in water and allowed to dry. The pulverised lapis luzuli was incorporated in a 'pastille' composed of linseed oil, wax, mastic, colophony, turpentine, etc, and the plastic mixture was left for a day or two before kneading in a basin of warm water. When the water became coloured with the blue which had sweated out of the 'pastille', the plastic lump was kneaded in a fresh vessel of warm water; this process being continued in new vessels until no more blue fell from the 'pastille'. The blue was allowed to settle in the vessels until the water could be poured away and the pigment allowed to dry. The finest and deepest blue would be found in the first vessel. The poorer ultramarine produced in the later vessels could be used in a fresh 'pastille' and kneaded in water to produce a smaller quantity of superior ultramarine[62].

There are frequent references in the literature of the period to 'liquid' gold and silver[63]. The term is misleading for gold and silver only become liquid when subjected to intense heat. The term 'liquid' was applied to impalpable powders of these metals which were fine enough to be bound with watercolour media and applied with the pen or brush. In principle they were used in the same way as other pigments although special processes were used to reduce the metals to powder, for the ordinary grinding process would have encouraged particles of soft metal to stick together. Although there are recipes which advise the artist to prepare his own gold and silver powders, even the earlier teatises generally advise the artist to purchase his gold and silver ready-made. 'If you will buye at the Potecaries shell gold or shell silver, with the which (being tempered with gume watter) you may verye well write with a pen, or painte with a pencell'[64].

---

62. Ibid., pp. 67–69.
63. e.g. Hilliard, p. 98.
64. Anon, *The Arte of Limming*, 1573, f.iv.

Hilliard had suggested that leaves of gold and silver could be reduced to powder by grinding them on a stone with honey and draining the honey away before mixing the powdered metals with gum water before painting. Perhaps the most important of the recipes for making powdered gold and silver is that which Norgate included in his first treatise:

> '... the manner of making Liquid Gould, which when yow have done, according to this ensuing direccon, yow will finde that Gould of your owne making infinitely to exceede any yow cann buy in bewty and quantaty.
>
> Take of your fine leafe Gould, about the Vallue of halfe a Crowne or Rather of the Cuttings of Gould to the same vallue, yow may have them at the Gould beaters, grinde this Gold with a thick and stronge Gume water, uppon a Reasonable large Stone, which yow must grinde very fine and paynefully, yow cann hardly Grinde it fine enough, it being rather *opus Laboris quam ingenii.* To make Gould thus, as yow grinde it still add more of your stronge Gum water, and though the Gould looke never soe black and durty, esteeme it not the lesse worth, but having brought it to a Computente finenesse, take it off from the Stone and putting it in a greate Shelle wash it cleane as yow are told in your former washings of Collours, Being very Cleane add to it a little quantaty of Mercury Sublimate on the pointe of your knife which yow must temper with it, and very little Gume to binde it in the Shell, and as it settles and begines to drye in the Shell shake it together and remove and spred the Gould about the sides of the Shell, that it may bee all together of one Colloure and fineness, when it is drye and fayre as it will bee if yow bee carefull to wash it cleane, use it with fayre water as yow doe your other Collours. And when yow have done this, yow will find your Gould much fayrar, and a greate deale more for mony, then yow cann buy.
>
> The same Course yow are to take with Liquid Silver which yow are to use in the same Manner'[65].

---

65. Norgate I, pp. 17–18.

Norgate repeated the recipe in his second treatise, but also noted that fine shell gold and silver were imported from Holland[66]. The term 'shell gold' is derived from the usual commercial presentation of gold (or silver) powder for watercolour painting, which was lightly bound with gum arabic and spread in a mussel shell ready for use. The author of the 'Hilliard Studio Manuscript' quoted the recipe from Norgate I saying, with characteristic honesty, that it was as he had been 'instructed by a manuscript' and adding that although he had tried the recipe it had produced liquid gold and silver 'but yet nothing so faire as I can buy neither so much for mony'[67].

Having in store a complete set of pigments, the next important task was to prepare the binders and additives to be used with them. The most important binder for watercolours then and now is gum arabic. However in the early sixteenth century some of the colours may have been bound with glair (the white of egg reduced to a transparent liquid by constant beating or sponging). The most convenient way to incorporate gum and glair with the pigments was to reduce them to a fine powder that could be mixed with the pigments and water in mussel shells before use. However glair was often used in its liquid form. Another important additive to the paint mixture was sugar candy (refined cane sugar) which was beaten to an impalpable powder and could be added to colours tending to crack when bound with gum alone[68]. The author of the 'Hilliard Studio Manuscript' also recommended the occasional addition of gum hedera to dispel bubbles in certain paint mixtures. Gum hedera is the exudation of the ivy vine; it was important that it should be kept in a tightly stoppered bottle because it could not be redissolved once it had become dry[69]. Powdered gum and sugar candy were frequently kept in ivory boxes and had to be stored in a dry place to prevent

66. Norgate II, p. 40.
67. Hilliard Studio MS., p. 62.
68. Ibid., p. 20.
69. Ibid., pp. 19–20.

congealing. The author of the 'Hilliard Studio Manuscript' suggested making a novel dispenser for these powders using a quill of a swan: '. . . you may cut two inches of the end of a quill (a swans quill is best because it is biggest) leaveing a little hole at the end and notched with little notches on the side (but not through the quill) to make the powder come out by scraping upon the notches with your naile, as Goldsmiths doe with there Borax boxes, And there must be a foote made of Ivory to stop it at the end where it was cutt of and whereon it must stand'[70] (Pl. 100).

Naturally the selection of brushes was of great importance to the limners and their concern is reflected in the treatises. The criteria for a good brush (which at that time was described as a 'pencil') were that it should be full and thick next to the quill descending to a sharp round point. It should not, as sometimes happened, divide into two points; and the hairs should be tight in the quill. The hairs used for miniature painting were either miniver, from the tails of ermine, or from calaber tails from certain species of squirrel[71]. In his second treatise Norgate said that the best pencils were made in London. The Hilliard Studio Manuscript gives valuable instructions for purchasing pencils and for those artists who wished to manufacture their own:

> 'The next that I thinke to commend unto your service are pensills, which if you buy, you must Choose such as are fast in the quills, Cleane sharpe and evenpointed, which you may try by moistning them in your mouth and squesing them flatt betwixt the thumb and forefinger of your left hand, which if it be fast in the Quill, and all the haires even of a length and levill, after you have so squesed it that pencill is good, otherwise no, . . . likewise if they be not devided into two parts as many times they doe, but full and thick next the quill, and soe discending into a round and sharp point

70. Ibid., p. 17.
71. See Murdoch, Murrell, Noon and Strong. *The English Miniature*, p. 214, note 46.

(but not long) which fashion for Limning I prefer before those that are long and slender as retaining the Colour and delivering it out more free and flowing then the other, and if you finde any haire longer than the rest, either take it away with a sharpe penknife or sisers that are sharpe, or pass it sudenly through the flame of a candle, but if you meete not with pensills to your mind, you may take Caliver tayls if you can gett them of which generally all our best pensills are made, they are much like unto the Tayls of our English Squirrils, but a much softer and finer furr. The tayle is joynted as many other furred tayles are. And the first joynt (viz. the tip end of the tayle) is not for makeing pensills on because the haires are Crooked bending towards the poynts, but all the other haire above that joynt is usefull which you must order on this manner. First take a paire of sharpe sisers, and clip of the haire of one tayle close by the roots, laying it down upon a Clean paper or table, and be sure to keep the small end of the haires all one way and also be carefull you do not Clip or Cutt the small ends but keep them natturally as they were. Than take a very small toothed Comb, which is clean (either made of the Tortoise shell or Ivory) and take up every clipping by itselfe, Combing the loose short haires away, saveing the longest which you hold fast by the small ends, betwixt the forefinger and the thumb of your left hand. When you have thus cleansed your haire very well lay it altogether on an even bord or table all the small ends one way; Then you must prepaire a Card or table booke leafe, rouling the haires within it like unto the socket of a Candlestick, yet to be open at both ends, then knock that end of the card, which hath the small points downwards very hard a pretty while, against an even board or stone by which means you shall settle all the small points of the haires to an equall evenness, which when you have perceived, unrole or open the card againe, and as the haires lay devide them asunder (with a penknifes point or the like) into as many parts as you intend to make pensills, great or less according to your occasions. But be sure to keep the poynts of the haires even as they were after you had sett them and so ty them up. The manner of a pensill knott shall hereafter be inserted. But if it should so fall out that you have occasion for very small pensills, and can gett none of these tayles aforementioned, then breake an ordinary pensill of fine haire observing how it is tyed up and fastned, and so takeing of the haire as much or as little as you please to make your pensill tie it together with a strong fine threed something loose at the first and round, fashioning it to an even poynt with laying and turning it round upon a cleane table or white paper, you must marke how the haires scatter and spreade, and with your penknife take a loose haire away now and then which you may safely doe the thread were-withall they are tyed being loose and slack; when it is to your minde tye it up faster. The manner of the knott how pensills are tyed is with a duble knott as is expressed in the Margent [unfortunately the marginal drawing has been omitted] putting the haire into the two nosses of the threed drawing little and little the two ends of the threed, loose at the first but when your pensill is fashioned as aforesaide draw it very hard, and so you shall tye it with such a knott, as will not undoe, then with the two ends of the threed tye it with such another knott a little lower then the former, and fitt them into quills according to the size of the pencill, also you must have prepared severall sticks according to the size of your severall quills to be cutt very even at both ends, for the thrusting your pensills down into the quill (For if you should putt them downe with an uneven stick or such a stick as is sharpe at the end you would spoyle your pensills.) when your pensills are thus made, dispose them upon handsome sticks of Ivory or Brassell Ebonie or the like of the length of an ordinary writing pen. . . . . Of these small pensills you are to have in a readiness six or seven for your severall Colours and shadowes in your worke besides some bigger pencills of severall sizes as your worke shall require. But remember that your pensills you use in gold workes and silver be ever reserved for that purpose onely, and not to mix or temper or worke other Colour with them. If any of your pensills be not small enough for your worke, then take Old Mr. Hilyards way (as he taught me) to make it small viz. wett your pensill in a Colour well gummed and when it is dry with a sharpe penkife you may cutt it round aboute as much or as little as you please, but not too much according to the sharpness you would have it, and when you wash it all the loose haires will wash away. And if your Colour will not runn to the end of the pensill Cutt or slip the end thereof a very little shorter, but be sure you cutt not too much, least you spoyle your pensill, It is requisite to increase your store with too great pensills (which you may make of the tip ends of your tayles which as aforementioned I tould you were not usfull) the one lightly to Brush of the dust from your Limnitures, the other to brush the dust from your shells of Colours when need requireth. You make these kind of dusting pensills of a pretty large-ness as tying six or eight of those joynts together for such pensills fitting them in pretty shafts, handsomly turned on purpose . . . And because pensills many times with long keeping are eaten with wormes and so spoyled for any good use, I will therefore in this place instruct you how to keep those pensills you doe not presently use from the wormes, that is by laying a few hopps among them by which meanes you shall preserve them from wormeating'[72].

The limner is now well supplied with pigments, gums and sugar candy to mix with them and an ample quantity of brushes, but assuming that he is already equipped with the paraphernalia for making pigments – the stones and muller, mortar and pestle, and various vessels – he needs a number of indispensible pieces of studio equipment before he can begin to paint. He requires a smooth slick stone and a burnisher made of a large dogs tooth for use in preparing the painting cards. The miniaturist normally worked at a small table fitted with drawers in which to store his dry pigments and colours on which he would place his desk or easel (Pl. 37). This usually had an upright angled face for the miniature and was often fitted with a drawer in the base for the shells of ready-mixed colour, pencils and cards. He made up his colours in clean mussel shells and used a large piece of mother-of-pearl or a horse mussel shell as a palette. The limner needed two glazed earthenware pots of clean water, one for taking up water to add to the colours and the other for washing the pencils. A pair of tweezers were useful for taking up hairs which might fall and stick to the wet paint. If the artist was to burnish his gold and silver he needed burnishers

72. Hilliard Studio MS., pp. 12–16.

made from small dog and weasel teeth neatly fitted into wooden handles. Finally a piece of paper was used both to protect the work from the brush-hand while painting and for testing the flow of paint from the pencil.

The preparation of the painting cards (or tables, as they were known) involved considerable care, cleanliness and neatness. From surviving examples of unfinished works it seems that these cards were made in a square or rectangular form and the circle or oval cut out when the work was completed. Selection of the basic materials was again of great importance; in Hilliard's words, '. . . knowe also that *Parchment* is the only goode and best thinge to limne one, but it must be virgine *Parchment*, such as never bore haire, but younge things found in the dames bellye, some calle it *Vellym*, some *Abertive* derived from the word *Abhortive*, for untimly birthe. It must be most finly drest, as smothe as any sattine . . .'[73]. The card used was a playing card[74] (Pl. 101) which on the plain white side (the backs of the cards were not decorated at that time) had to be smooth and free from dark specks. The author of the Hilliard Studio Manuscript has provided the most detailed description of the preparation of the painting tables:

> 'You must take ordinary cards but of the finest pastboard you can get without any specks on the white sides, and with a very smooth slickstone or a great tooth or the like polish and make them everywhere as smooth and as even as possablely you may on the white side thereof, or els wett the white side of your Card all over with a great pensill and soe soone as the water is sunke in burnish it smooth and hard on the other side laying the white side which was

73. Hilliard, pp. 94 and 96.

74. Although the manuscripts do not stipulate playing cards it is evident from an examination of the miniatures that this was the usual practice. Sanderson, whose book was largely a plagiarism of Norgate I, also made this clear in his instructions for preparing the vellum; he begins 'Take an ordinary playing Card. . .'. William Sanderson, *Graphice*, 1658, p. 59.

wett on a smooth Christall or Lookeing glass, or on a cleane and smooth grinding stone which is even; Then take abortive parchment the best you can get, and cut out a peice equall to the largness of your card, then take fine white and cleane starch that is cleanly made, and past if fast upon the Card after this manner, first lay your Abortive on a cleane paper, holding your Abortive at the fower corners, having one to helpe you, or else it will runn on a heape, then with a great fitched pensill take a little of the starch which must first be beaten or tempered on the palme of your hand with a knife, and spreade it thin on the Abortive, then take your card aforesaid and lay the white side thereof on the Abortive as close and as smooth as you can, or else you may spread on the starch with your knife over the card and instantly lay on the Abortive as even as you can, also take a slicked paper and lay it over the Abortive and rub it with your thumbe that it may be even on the card which soone put it into a booke and there let it rest, untill it be almost dry, and then lay the card thus pasted on a polished Christall or Lookeing glass, or on a cleane smooth and even stone that is without flawes or pitcholes the parchment side downewards, and holding it fast, with a great tooth or slick stone or the like burnish or polish the card as hard and as even as you may on the back side, by which meanes the other side whereon you are to worke will become very smooth, you must remember to past the nappy and inside of the said parchment to your card, and that the outside of your skin may be outwards, it being the smoother and better side to worke on although it be not so white. If you please to imitate a Landscape or History or that you will have your picture larger then a Card, you must then get sheets of pastbord whereof your finest Cards be made, and past your Abortive thereon as large as you please to make them and in the pasting of your cards or pastbord you must have a care that noe moats or dust get betweene the Abortive and the cards and that the cards and pastbord be without any spotts upon them for every small spott will be seene through the abortive'[75].

The first stage in painting a portrait miniature was to prepare

75. Hilliard Studio MS., pp. 37–9.

the painting card with a carnation ground on which to paint the features. Although it would approximate the complexion of the sitter the ground had to be very pale so that the carnation could stand for the highest lights in the features which were modelled with strokes of transparent paint. A well laid carnation was essential. The Hilliard Studio Manscript gives a full account of the method and the pitfalls awaiting the unwary:

> '.. take a card prepaired as aforesaid, and lay a ground or primer of flesh colour properly called a Carnation (which in no sort ought to have any glistering in it) and that you must temper in the shell with your finger, according to the complection of the party whose picture you make, if faire you must temper your complection with whit lead[76] and a little Red lead (which maketh the fairer carnation or complection) mingled together to a pretty quantity of an Indifferent thickness in a shell somewhat biger then ordinary; if the party be pale then lesser Red lead a little masticote amongst it, but if your complection be swarthy, or browne, then mingle white lead and red lead and a little fine masticote, or English Oker or both (or as old Mr. Hilyard did who put Oker de rouse in stead of English Oker) but be sure your ground or primer thus to be laid be ever fairer then the party whose picture you are to make, For though your ground be never so faire, yet in workeing you may darken or shadow it as much as you please, but if your ground be darke you can never heighten it or make it lighter, For Limning is but the shadowing of the same Colour your ground is of, therefore in Limning of pictures (I meane the naked part) you must never heighten it, but worke them downe to there just colour. Your ground and complection thus coloured and tempered, you must lay it over the card prepaired as aforesaid with a great pensill, in laying on this ground you must be very carefull to lay it as smooth and even as is possable and somewhat flowing that it dry not before your pensill least it seeme patched, and as cleane from spots, haires of the pensill

76. It should be noted that Horenbout, Holbein and Hilliard had used ceruse rather than white lead for this purpose.

or dust, as you can. In doeing of this you shall remember to fill your pensill full of colour rather thin and waterish then thick and gross and with two or three sweeps or dashes with a great pensill lay it in an instant, for the faster you doe it the better and the evener will the colour lye. And forget not to cover so much or more of your card then shall be needfull, and broader and larger then you meane to worke your face, because if you should happen to lay your ground too little, you will very hardly ad any more unto it, but very uneven and unsutable to the rest. Therefore all must be doone at once and speedily; if your colour will not take when you lay any ground, or the parchment be greasy (by reason of some sweaty hand or fingers that hath touched your parchment thereabouts) temper with your colour a little Eare wax[77], as little as may be. The same is very good to temper with the colours that peeles from the worke. And to prevent the saide greesiness touch not your worke; but if need be with a cleane pensill brush it or with a white feather (for a shift) wipe of the dust neither breath on it especially in Winter nor speake over your picture, without care for the least sparke or spitting will never be helped. You must remember that which I had almost forgott that is if your ground or Complection lyeth and be not to your mind you may lick it all of with your toung or wipe it of with a moist spunge, and after you have slicked the backside, lying the right side on a polished Christall or Lookeing glass as aforesaid, you may lay on your complection againe as you would have it, but use this way no oftner then necessity doth require, for often wetting your table or card can doe it no good, but rather the parchment will become rough or sometimes rise and come of from the Card or pastboard. The same inconvenience will sometimes happen if you be long in laying your Complection. I am the more particular in this description because I have seene your best workemen in this art oftentimes fayle in makeing or prepairing of the cards and laying of this ground, which will thus appeare by there pictures, if you veiw them by a contrary light, you shall finde them rough and unevenly wrought in many places, And not so neate and smooth

77. Earwax (cerumen) contains natural emulsifiers. See Murdoch, Murrell, Noon and Strong, *op. cit.*, p. 214, note 45.

> as when you behold them by a right light, or the same light it was wrought by'[78].

Perhaps the best practice was that of Hilliard and Oliver, who had a store of cards prepared with various carnation tones and would select one which was appropriate to the complexion of the sitter[79].

The account that follows of the sittings for a portrait miniature is distilled from the treatises of Norgate and the Hilliard Studio Manuscript. In discussing the treatment of the features these treatises describe the closer stippled handling characteristic of the later phase of Isaac Oliver's career (Pls. 96, 103), rather than the spare schematic treatment of Nicholas Hilliard who would have needed far less time in which to paint the face.

The description is general – each artist adopted variations. Holbein, for example, probably never painted a miniature from life but worked from preliminary drawings and notations.

The artist's desk would be placed so that the light fell across it from left to right; a simple expedient to prevent the shadow of the painting hand from covering the work. (A left-handed painter, such as Holbein, would have adopted the contrary procedure.) The sitter, placed some two yards in front of the artist for a head and shoulders portrait or six yards for a full-length, was invariably illuminated from the left with the right side of his features to the light.

In the first sitting, lasting from two to four hours, the limner was concerned with the first broad working in the features and with freely washing in the hair (Pl. 102). The artist would take small quantities of the colours needed to mix the flesh tones of the features, placing them around the circumference of his mother-of-pearl palette. The mixtures suggested were lake, red lead and a little white for the cheeks and lips, indigo and white for blue shadows, English ochre, indigo and a little pink or masticot for the faint grey-blue

---

78. Hilliard Studio MS., pp. 40–42.
79. Norgate II, p. 20.

half-tones, and for the deep shadows, English ochre, umber and white; although for the harder shadow tones of men's faces lake, pink and umber were used. These were only suggested mixtures and the artist would use his discretion in mixing the colour-tones for a particular portrait. As Norgate said '. . . to prescribe an absolute and generall Rule in this is Impossible, Nature soe infinitely varieth in the Collour and Shaddowes of all faces'[80].

The practice of adding white to most of the flesh tones may seem slightly curious. How do we reconcile Norgate's advocacy of transparency, '. . . ffor in Lymning Pictures yow must never heighten, but worke them downe to theire Just Collour'[81] with his later exhortation, '. . . remember that in all or most of the shadowes white is ever a dayly guest, and seldome absent but in the deepest shadowes'[82]? The answer to this proposition is quite simple. The amounts of white added to the colours were minute; sufficient to make the strokes blend softly with the carnation but not large enough to make them opaque.

At the beginning of the sitting the artist drew the outlines of the face over the carnation using a fine pencil and a very faint rose colour made from lake mixed with white, or with some of the carnation colour. This colour was so faint that if a mistake was made it could be corrected with a slightly stronger colour and still not be apparent when working the flesh tones. Although Hilliard would have been content with a pure line drawing of the profile and major features, Norgate said that the shadows of the face should also be marked in this first faint drawing to serve as an *aide memoire* when working the flesh tones[83]. Hilliard made it abundantly clear in this treatise that the basis for the whole drawing was the most significant contour of the face: '. . . yor marke shalbe your first line which you

---

80. Norgate I, pp. 9–10.
81. Ibid., p. 9.
82. Norgate II, p. 22.
83. Norgate I, p. 10.

drawe, but that must be most truly drawne, for the lyne must be a scalle to all the rest and let that yor first lyne be the forehead stroake, as for exampel soe then yo shall proceed by that scalle or scantlinge to doe all proportionablye to that bignes, as if the forehead be but so longe, then the rest of that lyne to the Chine is but twice so long, as thus, and so proceed still, weel marking when yo loosse that line, that is to say, when that lyne is not to you, to your seeing, as when yo first sawe it, and drue it for then your mark is remembred, which yo shall best knowe and perceive by the distance betwene the eye and that lyne, which also yo must mark howe it was when yo drwee that lyne, howe neare it or howe fare'[84]. However at least one of Hilliard's pupils disagreed with this rule: 'Old Mr. Hilyards way was to draw the forehead stroake first and according to proportion the face. But I allwayes drawe the eyes first leaving the distance of an eye betweene the two eyes, or according as the life is, and proportion of the face thereunto. But let everyone please himselfe in his begining, soe his ending be truly done according to the life'[85].

When the limner was satisfied with his line drawing of the face he could go on to draw the posture with a stronger colour before proceeding to dead-colour the features (Pl. 102). The dead-colouring required a reasonably large pencil working broadly, 'after the manner of wasshing or hatching, drawing your pencell alonge with faynte and gentle strokes . . . not caringe to bee exacte and Curious, but rather bould and Judicious, for I have seene Pictures done by a good Hand (I meane begoone and dead collored only) that though neare at hand they seemed exceeding Rough, uneaven, and unplesent, yet being held and receaved at a little distance from the Eye, they appeare very smothe, neate and delicat'[86]. The tones of the face were worked in, not bothering to cover the carnation completely. They were applied loosely in their proper places to achieve a rough likeness of

84. Hilliard, p. 80.
85. Hilliard Studio MS., p. 56.
86. Norgate I, p. 12.

the sitter and an impression of the planes and modelling of the face. The work advanced evenly so that no part was more finished than the rest. Towards the end of the sitting the hair could be drawn and roughly washed in a middle-tone. Finally the painter would fill in any places in the face where the carnation was not covered and deepen the shadows.

The second sitting could take six hours or more to complete. The main work was in refining the dead-colouring of the features, using a smaller pencil and the same tones as before, '. . . working, driving and sweetning the same Collours one into another, to the end that noething be lefte in your worke with a Harde edge or uneaven heape or patch of Collours, but all soe swepte and driven one into an other with the poynte of somewhat a sharper pencell then you used at first, as that your Shadowes may lye soft and smothe, being dispersed and gently extended into and towards the lighter parts of the ffACE like ayre or vapory smoke'[87]. This description fits the later face-painting of Isaac Oliver, adopted and continued by his son, Peter (Pl. 96). After about two hours the work on the features would have progressed sufficiently for the limner to lay his background and put in the basic grounds for the costume and ruff or collar (Pl. 102).

The blue bice and ultramarine used in backgrounds were heavy and crystalline; difficult to use as watercolours. A special procedure was needed for these paints to lay flat and even in the finished work. The difficulty is highlighted in Norgate's account of the method:

> 'If Blewe yow must lay it thus (and harde it is to lay it well and even your *Bise* being puer, and Cleane washed, temper as much in a Shell as will Cover a Carde, lett it be all throughly moyste and well bound with Gume. then with a smale pencell goe about the sayd Collour the umstroke or Porfoile, I meane the outermost lyne and masterstroke of the ffACE and body of the said Picture; That

87. Ibid., p. 13.

done with a greate pencell wash over somewhat Carelesly the whole ground that yow meane to Cover with somewhat a thinn and water-ish Blewe: And with a Reasonable greate pencell full of Collour and flowing lay over that very place, with a thicke and substanciall body of Colloure, which before yow had only washed over. In the doeing of this yow must be very swifte, keeping the Collour moiste that yow have layd; not suffering any parte thereof to drye till all be Covered. By this meanes it will lye eaven smoth as glasse, and the wetting the Carde over before with the thinn Collour makes the rest that yow lay after to settle even and hansomly which otherwise would lye in heapes like unto drifte sand'[88].

By the time Norgate wrote his second treatise in the middle of the seventeenth century the background was normally laid with 'darke and sad colour, to sett of the picture'[89]. No doubt Norgate's 'darke and sad' colours were those which Samuel Cooper favoured during the earlier years of his independent career in the 1640s. These dark brown-black grounds were executed in exactly the same floating method used for blue backgrounds.

The other type of ground was that which represented a crimson satin or velvet curtain[90]. There were three variants of the curtain ground, all invented by Nicholas Hilliard. The earliest, which appeared as if freshly laundered and ironed, hung in neat squares behind the sitter as in the first dated miniature where this convention appears, the *Sir Henry Slingsby* at the Fitzwilliam Museum[91] (Pl. 56). Hilliard may have been influenced by the oil miniature painted on gold of *Mary I* by Hans Eworth (Pl. 105).

A little later Hilliard adopted a second manner where the crim-son cloth was draped as if it were a curtain hung behind the sitter.

88. Ibid., pp. 13–14.
89. Norgate II, p. 34.
90. Ibid., p. 35.
91. Although in that miniature the curtain was draped as were the curtains of Hilliard's second manner.

Norgate describes the technique: 'If yow would have your Ground Crimson like Satten, yow must with India Lake marke out, where and in what places yow will have those stronge and hard lights and refleccons to faule, which is seene in Satten or Velvett. There lay your lights with a thinn and waterish *Lake*, and while it is wett with a stronger and darker Collour of Lake thicke ground, lay in deepnings and hard stronge Shaddowes close by the other lights'[92] (Pl. 104). After the accession of James I Hilliard adopted another method for painting these crimson curtains possibly because he was bored with the constant repetitions of royal portraits. However, although the method was a short cut to a similar effect, it did produce a crispness which may have appealed to Hilliard as more suited to his abstract, decorative approach to miniature painting (Pl. 106). The inconsistency of these lake backgrounds with the descriptions of their method of execution offered by Norgate is resolved by the Hilliard Studio Manuscript: 'Old Mr. Hilyard did use to lay the ground aforesaid thick with lake, and while it was wett, with a cleane dry pensill would wipe away the Colour againe by drawing his pensill hard all along where he would have the heightning of the red vellvet appeare and the strong reflection will be this way very well and speedily expressed'[93]. After the background the grounds for the ruff and costume were laid flatly with an opaque middle tone. The features, which had been painted against the white background of the vellum, would appear pale and lifeless. The limner would spend the remainder of the second sitting working over them again, paying particular attention to the strong shadows, and working over the hair, darkening it with transparent colour and adding the necessary heightenings with opaque paint. After this six hour sitting '. . . the Pictured gone, or weary with sitting (as commonly they are)'[94] the artist could, at his leisure, go over his work,

92. Norgate I, p. 14.
93. Hilliard Studio MS., p. 52.
94. Norgate I, p. 15.

polishing and finishing any part which did not require direct observation from nature.

The third and final sitting involved the finishing touches. The ruff or collar would be painted over the middle-tone ground with transparent grey and white, and the costume heightened and shadowed. The features would be worked over very carefully observing facial characteristics. Finally, any armour, gold jewellery, pearls, diamonds and other stones would be made. For the armour a flat ground of silver paint was laid, burnished and shaded with a mixture of silver, indigo, litmus and a little umber, leaving the burnished silver ground for the highlights. If the armour was gilded, the ground was laid with English ochre and gold, or with the yellow stone from an ox gall mixed with gold and deepened with black in the deepest shadows, and heightened with burnished gold paint. Embossed goldworks, such as those which represented the settings for precious stones, were raised on the surface of the vellum by 'raysing in those Heigh and Round places *Inoncion* or heape of the Gaule stone, or English Oker, by often touching with a Pencell full of Collour; and resting the poynte of it in one and the same place till your heape or touches be arraysed above your other work. That done, Cover over your Raysed worke with Gould, and yow shall find it exceeding fayre and bright. . .'[95]. Hilliard gives us a thorough description of the method of painting pearls: 'The pearles layed with a whit mixed with a littel black, a littel Indy [indigo] blewe, and a littel masticot, but very littel in comparison of the whit, not the hundred parte. That being dry, give the light of your *Pearle* with silver some what more to the light side then the shadowe side, and Round and full as yo cane, then take good whit delayed with a littel *Masticot*, and underneath at the shadowe side give it a Compassing stroke which showes the reflection that a *Pearle* hath then without that a smale Shadowe of Seacole undermost of all'[96]. The silver highlight of the

95. Ibid., p. 17.
96. Hilliard, p. 98.

pearl was burnished with the tooth of a weasel or some other small animal. Diamonds were painted with lines and black shading (to express the cut of the stone) over a burnished silver ground left exposed to represent the highlights. Hilliard was reluctant to divulge the technique for representing coloured gemstones. In his treatise he said: 'A word I praye yo tuchinge the making of those beautifull rubies or other stones, how yo soe arteficially doe them, that being never so littel they seme precious *stones* naturall, cleere and perspicious, soe that (by your favor) is no parte of *limning*, wherefore requier it not, it appertaineth merly to ane other arte. And though I use it in my limming, it is but as a mayson or Joyner, when he hath done his worke, and cane also paynt or guilde his freeses and needful parts therof'[97]. Later Hilliard relents and gives a brief and somewhat misleading account of the method: '. . . other stones must be glased uppon the Silver with their proper cullors with some varnish etc.'[98]. In his first treatise Norgate was only able to give the recipe in cipher. The 'Herogliphicall and Cabalistick Caractors' which compose the cipher are, as Martin Hardie pointed out in his Introduction to 'Miniatura' (Norgate II), simply a transposed alphabet where a = n, b = o, etc., and the recipe was given in plain language in both the Hilliard Studio Manuscript and Norgate's later Treatise. In order to make these counterfeit precious stones a ground of silver was laid and burnished to provide a reflector. A transparent pigment suitable to the colour of the stone was then mixed with turpentine resin. The mixture was then taken up with a heated iron needle and laid and modelled to the required shape and thickness over the silver. The pigments for making the different stones were India Lake for rubies, verdigris and turmeric for emeralds, and ultramarine for sapphires[99]. India lake and Indigo were used to make an Amethyst. The author of the Hilliard Studio Manuscript said that he had seen

97. Ibid., p. 94.
98. Ibid., p. 98.
99. Norgate I, p. 17.

particoloured Agates which he thought were executed in this technique but which were not transparent[100]. The technique was also used to represent enamelling on jewels and picture boxes. If the turpentine took rather long to dry a little powder of clarified mastic varnish could be added. According to Norgate, Hilliard was in the habit of coating exposed silver with garlic juice to prevent it from tarnishing[101], but judging from the blackened condition of the silver in the majority of his miniatures the method was not effective.

Having completed the costume and added the jewellery the third and last sitting was at an end. Doubtless the miniaturist would have retained the miniature in order to flourish any gold inscription.

There were occasions when the artist would have been obliged to work away from his studio and be forced to improvise. Queen Elizabeth, for example, was unlikely to make progress to the tenement in Gutter Lane in order to sit for Master Hilliard. We are indebted to the author of the Hilliard Studio Manuscript, the only contemporary writer to mention working outside the studio, for his detailed instructions for making a pocket painting box, which may reflect Hilliard's own practice in such cicumstances:

> 'And because you should not be unfurnished with things necessary to take a picture from home as well as at home, be pleased to have in rediness such a Box as I contrived for myselfe, of six inches Long and three inches broad and two inches deepe, that you may Carry it in your pocket the inside of your Lid must be Laid aCross with four penny or six penny greene Taffety ribbin, the whole length thereof beginning at the hinges laying the ribin a little one over another, fastning the ribbin on the sides and Covering the outsides with red Leather, gilded if you please. The box being open and the lid thereof turned quite backwards the lid is then a desk to limme upon and the ribbin is for sticking your pictures in when you worke them. There must be alsoe a stiff wyer stuck fast and upright in the inside

100. Hilliard Studio MS., p. 61.
101. Norgate I, p. 18.

of the box at the bottom halfe the breadth of your bigest pensill stick from one of the sides to put on your pensills whose stickes must have holes for that purpose and pencills at each end, and not above the length of the box within, so that the haire and points of your pensills be not hurt against the ends of your Box within; Your Box thus made as is here exprest (Pl. 107), you must not be unfurnished with three of four peices of Bayse, or the like of the length, and breadth of the Box within to lay between your shells of Colours to keepe them from stirring and fridging in the Box. It is very fitting also to make a case (if I may so call it) of two white Cards put together the white sides inwards with a Ring of fine Vellem or thin parchment, and with a little starch fasten the edges together on each side, and at one end leaveing the other end open to put in your picture whilst your are a workeing, either halfe way or a quarter, as it pleaseth you, so that by this means you need not handle or finger your picture whereby any greasiness might Come unto it to hinder your Colours from workeing upon it. You may have two or three of these cases of severall biggnesses proportionable to the pictures you meane to limne'[102].

102. Hilliard Studio MS., pp. 10–11.

INDEX

References to Plates are shown in italic

Index

Index

Index

Index

Index